MORE THAN A WOMB

MORE THAN A WOMB

*Childfree Women in the Hebrew Bible
as Agents of the Holy*

Lisa Wilson Davison

CASCADE *Books* · Eugene, Oregon

MORE THAN A WOMB
Childfree Women in the Hebrew Bible as Agents of the Holy

Cascade Books
An Imprint of Wipf and Stock Publishers
199 W. 8th Ave., Suite 3
Eugene, OR 97401

www.wipfandstock.com

PAPERBACK ISBN: 978-1-62032-953-5
HARDCOVER ISBN: 978-1-4982 -8551-3
EBOOK ISBN: 978-1-7252-4847-2

Cataloguing-in-Publication data:

Name: Davison, Lisa Wilson, author.

Title: More than a womb : childfree women in the Hebrew Bible as agents of the holy / Lisa Wilson Davison.

Description: Eugene, OR: Cascade Books, 2021. | Includes bibliographical references and index.

Identifiers: ISBN: 978-1-62032-953-5 (paperback). | ISBN: 978-1-4982-8551-3 (hardcover). | ISBN: 978-1-7252-4847-2 (ebook).

Subjects: LSCH: Women in the Bible. | Bible. Old Testament—Criticism, interpretation, etc.

Classification: BS1199.W7 D40 2021 (print). | BS1199 (ebook).

07/29/21

This book is dedicated to women who, by choice or circumstance, are not mothers and have experienced shaming by others that they are somehow not fully a woman. You are enough.

CONTENTS

ACKNOWLEDGMENTS

No book is the product of just one person's labor. I would like to thank Cascade Books and my editor, Dr. K. C. Hanson, for giving me a chance to publish this book that has been in my heart for far too long. I also want to acknowledge the late Dr. Dennis E. Smith for encouraging me to submit the proposal for the book. My progress would have been much slower if it were not for Dr. Eileen Campbell-Reed, who served as my writing coach and accountability partner in the final leg of this journey. I am grateful for Alexis Engelbrecht-Villafane, my research assistant, who helped me with the details of the book in so many ways. My employer, Phillips Theological Seminary, granted me two six-month sabbaticals to focus on the writing project. I am grateful for all of my colleagues who supported me during this process, especially the original members of the Women's Writing Group: Dr. Ellen Blue, Rev. Belva Jordan, Dr. Mindy McGarrah Sharp, Dr. Sarah Morice Brubaker, and Dr. Nancy C. Pittman. This book would not be possible without my life companion, Rev. Michael A. Davison Jr. He is the true embodiment of a supportive spouse, cheering me on and reminding me that I did have something worth sharing with readers.

INTRODUCTION

A Story

While it may not seem that not being a mother should be a big deal in our postmodern twenty-first century world, you would be surprised at the negative reactions I receive from folks when they learn that I do not have children: they range from pity to outright disgust. Certainly, the church is one of the realms where I receive the most negative responses from well-meaning people who indicate what a shame it is that I will never know the joy (and the pain) of being a parent. However, even in the secular and scientific world my decision is viewed as selfish or even unnatural. When my companion and I decided to finalize our decision not to have children, he spoke to his doctor about getting a vasectomy. The physician responded that he was much too young (under forty) to make such a permanent choice. My doctor, likewise, advised me to wait because I could (or perhaps would) change my mind. Eventually, when he was thirty-eight, my husband found a urologist who would perform the procedure. We have never regretted our choice.

When the local paper in the town where we lived ran a story about our decision to be what it called "childless by choice," the reporter sent to interview us asked how we could reconcile our choice with the Bible's teaching that children are a blessing from God, referencing Ps 127:3. She didn't acknowledge verse 4, where the psalmist describes sons as arrows in their father's quiver—an image evoking the fragility of life in the ancient world. Obviously the newspaper reporter did not realize or remember that I teach the Hebrew Bible for a living. The reporter went on to inquire about whether we were worried that without children we would not have anyone to take care of us in our old age. And I am the one who is considered selfish? Not to pick on an unknowing newspaper reporter, some of my friends who would consider themselves enlightened and feminist, and who have children of their own, indicate that I have missed out on some necessary experience for me to be a fulfilled woman. Clearly there is something wrong with me. But as Betty Rollins puts it, "Women have child-bearing equipment. For them to choose not to use the equipment is no more blocking what is instinctive than it is for a man who, muscles or no, chooses not to be a weightlifter."[1]

My experience is not unique. I have heard similar stories from other women who are not mothers about being judged harshly for not having known the "joy" and "fulfillment" of being a mom. The association of "true womanhood" with motherhood is prevalent in the United States even with our twenty-first-century "wokeness" about sexuality and gender. Even I have been influenced by the presumption that whatever I do accomplish must fit within the broad category of "reproduction." In the preface to my first book, *Preaching Women of the Bible*, I wrote these words, "While writing the book has felt like birthing a beloved child, the book's completion does not mean the end of this phase of study. There are too many women whose stories have yet to be studied and preached. This book is but my firstborn."[2] When I wrote the book, my companion and I had already decided not to have children, yet the only vocabulary I had for describing the writing process evoked the birthing of children. With these words, I had unintentionally "motherized" myself. "Motherize" is a word that I use (and probably coined) to describe the process by which a woman who is not a mother is made to become like a mother so that others feel more comfortable. This has happened to me numerous times in churches, where on Mother's Day "all mothers" are recognized (usually by receiving a flower), and I'm included because no one knows what to do with me and others like me. While those who recognize "all mothers" have good intentions for the most part, I am not a mother and have no desire to be treated like a mother.

Studying and Teaching Women of the Hebrew Bible

One of the difficulties in studying the women of the Hebrew Bible with a feminist perspective (seeing women as equal with men) is the male focus within the ancient texts. Most female characters in the stories are identified

---

1. Quoted in Cain, *The Childless Revolution*, 147.
2. Davison, *Preaching the Women of the Bible*, 7.

by their relationships to males. They are mothers, wives, daughters, sisters, and concubines. While I am intentional in focusing on the women, the spotlighting of men in the biblical stories, along with the sexism of the twenty-first century, has shaped me in ways that for quite some time I did not recognize. The first few times I taught a course on women in the Hebrew Bible, the syllabus was arranged by grouping women as mothers, wives, daughters, sisters, and other women. When I finally saw how my course was reinforcing this male bias, I was shocked and disappointed. The next syllabus was completely revised to present the stories of the Hebrew Bible by following a female chronology.

Sexism and stereotypes continued to show up in unexpected ways as I taught about women. My practice has been to ask students to name their favorite female character from the Hebrew Bible. After recognition by some that they really didn't know the names of female characters, their answers usually included some of the more obvious women: Ruth, Naomi, Miriam, Sarah, Rachel, Rebekah, and so forth. I remember one time when a student said their favorite character was Deborah, and my first response was to say that I really did not like Deborah. When I was asked for a reason, I said I do not really like her because she acts "like a man." As the words came out of my mouth, I could not believe what I was hearing. Where did I, a proud feminist, get the idea that fighting or engaging in violence, or both are male behaviors and not appropriate for females?

The purpose of sharing these stories is to make clear that everyone is shaped by cultural ideals and stereotypes about women and men, despite their best intentions not to be. Identifying incidents within my life and scholarship is to assure readers that I am not judging others' interpretations of female characters in the Hebrew Bible without admitting my own shortcomings. As all biblical interpreters do, each scholar brings a perspective shaped by their reading location and contributes in new ways to our understanding of texts. What I offer in this book is another possible lens through which we can read the stories of women in the Hebrew Bible, with particular attention to female characters who are not framed by their reproductive potential or failure. By no means is this the only or even best interpretation of the texts; however, this angle does contribute to our ongoing conversations about the Hebrew Bible and issues of biological sex and gender identity. Hopefully, it is a new and helpful offering.

This book lifts up women who, working with the Divine, play amazing roles in the stories of Israel: they are prophets, judges, worship leaders, warriors, scholars, and scribes; they help people celebrate their God's triumph over oppression; they speak boldly to those in power; they go into battle to secure their people's safety; they give wise judgments in important legal matters; they authenticate texts and inspire reform to help Israel return to the way of Torah. In ways that were not tied to their wombs/fertility, they make Israel's story possible and help it to continue to future generations.

For Whom Is This Book Intended?

The most obvious answer would be that this book is for those who wish to study the women in the Hebrew Bible. Particularly, though, the gleanings from the study that follows are for women, who by choice or circumstance, are not mothers and are seeking a way to claim a place in the stories of their faith. Perhaps, like me, they are tired of being judged by others for what is seen as a lack or of being "motherized" so that their lives align with others' concepts of womanhood. This book is also for anyone frustrated by having their identity defined by whether or not they put their reproductive organs to use and have children. Ultimately, what I present here is for everyone who holds the stories of the Hebrew Bible as important to their faith and wishes to expand their own ideas about sexuality and gender identity. Whatever your reason for reading the book may be, my wish is that you will find the material enlightening and the time you invest in it well spent.

1

MOTHERHOOD IN THE HEBREW BIBLE

Introduction

The Hebrew Bible contains confusing and often contradictory messages about many different issues (e.g., sacrifice, war, the nature of God, and so forth), but there seems to be one message that is perfectly clear: a woman's main purpose in life is to bear children, specifically to birth sons. *Her Role then + Now* With the first recorded commandment given by God to the first woman and man, "be fruitful and multiply" (Gen 1:28), fertility in the newly created world is given primary importance. The necessity of procreation is reiterated through the multiple stories about barren women and the lengths to which they are willing to go in order to give their husbands sons. In the garden of Eden story, this emphasis on procreation is named as an inevitable part of the woman's future, "To the woman (the Lord God) said, 'I will greatly increase your pangs in childbearing; in pain you shall bring forth children, yet your desire shall be for your husband, and he shall rule over you'" (Gen 3:16). Although the translation of this verse has been greatly debated, the obligation of bearing children is unambiguous. According to the biblical writers, the possibility of a woman dying without having fulfilled her role as a mother is truly a fate worse than death. Consider the story of the sacrifice of the daughter of Jephthah in Judges 11. According to the storyteller(s), the real tragedy involved in the violent end of this young life is summarized by the statement. "She had never slept with a man" (Judg

1

11:39). This point is expressed also in the punishment of David's wife Michal for her chastising the king's unbecoming behavior when the ark of the covenant is brought into Jerusalem. "And Michal the daughter of Saul had no child to the day of her death" (2 Sam 6:23).

This perspective on true womanhood also is found in the New Testament. The theme of a barren wife is continued in the story of Elizabeth (Luke 1:7), her miraculous pregnancy, and the birth of John the Baptist. In the epistles, an equally strong, even strident, expression of the requirement for women to become mothers is found in 1 Tim 2:15: "Yet she will be saved through childbearing, provided they continue in faith and love and holiness, with modesty." This antiwoman theology (and patriarchal requirement of motherhood) is carried forward in the Christian tradition by the so-called church fathers. Saint Augustine wrote in a letter to a friend: "I fail to see what use woman can be to man, if one excludes the function of bearing children."[1] The leader of the Protestant Reformation, Martin Luther, put it even more bluntly: "If they [women] become tired or even die, that does not matter. Let them die in childbirth, that's why they are there."[2]

These troubling viewpoints continue even into the twenty-first century. Albert Mohler, president of Southern Baptist Theological Seminary in Louisville, Kentucky, wrote in a blog post from February 2009, "The church should insist that the biblical formula calls for adulthood to mean marriage and marriage to mean children. This reminds us of our responsibility to raise boys to be husbands and fathers and girls to be wives and mothers."[3] In full disclosure, it is not only men who have espoused these views that womanhood is most fully expressed in motherhood. Well-known humorist and newspaper columnist Erma Bombeck had this to say: "It is not until you become a mother that your judgment slowly turns to compassion and understanding."[4]

With these overt messages bombarding women today, how do those who are unable to have children or who choose not to have children, by biology or by adoption, understand themselves in relation to this motherhood-centered concept of womanhood, which seems to have the full support of the Bible and God? For the approximately 12 percent of US women between twenty-five and forty-four who experience some form of

1. Quoted in Armstrong, *The Gospel according to Woman*, 61.
2. Quoted in Armstrong, *The Gospel according to Woman*, 69.
3. Mohler, "Deliberate Childlessness."
4. Bombeck, *Motherhood*, 10.

impaired (fecundity,[5] being physically unable to bear a child) often causes feelings of despair or guilt; some even entertain a belief that God is punishing them (often citing the biblical idea of God closing a woman's womb). The increasing numbers of women who choose never to become mothers are often condemned as unfaithful at best and sinful at worst. Mohler made this judgment very clear in the same blog post (mentioned above), writing, "Willful barrenness and chosen childlessness must be named as moral rebellion."[6] Can another understanding of a woman's worth, besides motherhood, be found in the Hebrew Bible? There are female characters in the biblical texts who are never described as mothers yet who make important contributions to the story. Can these women provide an alternative understanding of womanhood within these ancient Scriptures?

This book explores the stories about women in the Hebrew Bible who are never described as fulfilling their maternal destiny and yet who are not labeled as barren. Attention will be given specifically to Miriam, Deborah, Jael, Huldah, and Esther along with consideration of unnamed women also not identified as mothers (e.g., the medium of Endor, the wise women of Tekoa and Abel). Why are they not described in the same way as Sarah or Hannah, for example? Why is this supposed lack in their lives not seen as problematic? Is there a difference between a woman who is barren and one who is childfree?[7]

Certainly the possibility exists that any woman mentioned in the Hebrew Bible did have children who are not mentioned in the text but within the world of the story they are childless. Without a biological or divine explanation for this fact, the literary possibility exists that their not being mothers was judged not to be a problem but perhaps a choice, a blessing, or both. Given their roles in the Hebrew Bible, these women's lack of children seems to provide them with opportunities not available to women with children, to mothers. More importantly, though, the vital roles childfree

---

5. Statistics taken from Center for Disease Control and Prevention, "Infertility FAQs."

6. Mohler, "Deliberate Childlessness."

7. The term *childfree* is used intentionally to avoid the negative connotations of *childless*, which implies that a woman is lacking because she does not fill the role of mother. *Childfree* has been used widely in contemporary circles of persons who have chosen not to reproduce. In fact, self-identified childfree communities exist for the purpose of providing both support for those who are not parents (and face negative reactions from society because of their status) and an opportunity for childfree persons to make connections with others who share this characteristic.

women play in Israel's story are remembered without the women's being identified as biological mothers.

Mothers, Mothers: Seeing Mothers Everywhere

In the early efforts to lift up women in the stories of the Hebrew Bible, most feminist scholars began with a reconsideration of the role of mothers. Given that it is in this role that the majority of female biblical characters appear in the stories, this is a natural place to start. It is also a much-needed step in the endeavor to correct the male bias not only of the biblical writers but also of biblical interpretation. The Hebrew Bible is written in a way that forces readers to focus on the male characters in the stories and only to notice any female as she relates to the lives of these men. The androcentric emphases of the texts make it nearly impossible not to do this. While the most obvious example of this bias might be the high number of unnamed women in the Hebrew Bible who are merely described as a man's mother, wife, or daughter, even named women tend to be in a story, at best, in supporting roles to the male characters, many times as antagonists or simply as extras in the scene. For example, see the role of Dinah in Gen 34 or Bathsheba's presence in David's story (2 Sam 11).

Yet, particularly in Genesis, the matriarchs are undeniably prominent characters in the stories about Israel's earliest beginnings. Sarah's taking control of the situation to address Abraham's lack of an heir, which she exercises as a result of God's failing to keep covenant, is a clear example of how much influence a woman can have in the biblical story. Still, Sarah is ultimately the one who is controlled by being forced to have a child in her nineties. There is no denying that Rebekah overshadows the character of Isaac in the second generation of the ancestors. She is in charge and actively controls the situation so that the son of God's choosing receives the blessing from her husband. Again, though, she is a mere cog in the great engine of a patriarchal and patrilineal story. We read about Rachel and Leah, who are forced into a fierce sibling rivalry by a conniving father and a culture that valued women based solely on their ability to produce sons; neither of these mothers gets what she wants. Leah never wins Jacob's love, and Rachel dies while giving birth to just her second son. Yes, motherhood is a way for women at least to have some power, but they still function to further male rules and desires.

I appreciate and have contributed to the important work done by feminist scholars on the reclaiming of the stories of the biblical mothers; however, I would like to suggest that in our zeal to find an important role for women, we have been complicit in the patriarchal system of continuing to limit a woman's worth to the biological role of motherhood. One example of this is Leila Bronner's book *Stories of Biblical Mothers: Maternal Power in the Hebrew Bible*, in which she identifies different categories of mothers and deals with each in a chapter. I am not suggesting that there is anything wrong with her approach, but I do take issue with one chapter, titled "Metaphorical Mothers." In it, Bronner deals with women like Deborah and Miriam (as well as others), whom she identifies as "not biological mothers" before going on to show how they "become symbolic mothers through their outstanding devotion to their people."[8] Essentially, Bronner reinterprets the important roles of these women as forms of what she calls "mothering," which she claims "becomes a style of leadership, which differs significantly from how their male colleagues govern their people."[9] Thus, Miriam has many "mothering qualities" as she co-mothers Moses. In citing the reference to Miriam in Mic 6:4, Bronner claims, "Miriam is the nurturing female figure in the triad of Israel's leaders."[10] She openly admits to excluding the story in Num 12, where Miriam appears to be anything but the encourager of Moses. Huldah is read as "a maternal figure, [who] offers guidance to an entire people . . . and presents consolation to King Josiah, mothering him in a time of national crisis."[11] Bronner even manages to make the "Witch of Endor" into a "metaphorical mother, devotedly caring" for King Saul.[12]

In her book *Warrior, Dancer, Seductress, Queen*, Susan Ackerman, relying on work by Claudia Camp, spends time addressing the title, "a mother in Israel," applied to Deborah in Judg 5 (which will be covered in Chapter 5). After concluding that this label is not meant to be taken as a biological description, Ackerman goes on to claim that certain "motherly" characteristics are present in Deborah (i.e., she is a good and effective counselor who uses her skills to protect the "heritage" of YHWH, and she shows a willingness to step forward as a military commander to lead her

8. Bronner, *Stories of Biblical Mothers*, xii–xiii.

9. Bronner, *Stories of Biblical Mothers*, 83.

10. Bronner, *Stories of Biblical Mothers*, 84.

11. Bronner, *Stories of Biblical Mothers*, 88.

12. Bronner, *Stories of Biblical Mothers*, 91.

people for the sake of unity and peace).[13] Then, later in the book, Ackerman applies these same criteria to Judith, and declares her to be "like Deborah in her 'maternal' role."[14] Although Judith seems to be a clear case of a woman who never had children, she has now been "motherized" by well-meaning feminist scholars, as if that is the only way that she can be understood as an important female figure, something that the male bias of the biblical writers does not even need to do.

Some scholars assume biological motherhood for female biblical characters even without any evidence to make such an assumption. This can be seen in the work of those who draw the conclusion that the wise woman of Tekoa was a mother, even though her portrayal of a mother is only part of her prophetic parable to convince David to reconcile with his son Absalom (2 Sam 14:1–24). Similarly, the wise woman of Abel is said to have drawn from her experiences as a mother when she addresses Joab in defense of her city (2 Sam 20:14–22). The implication is that she could not have done this without having had the actual experience of being a biological mother.[15] This same assumption that all women were biological mothers is found in Phyllis Bird's now classic work, *Missing Persons and Mistaken Identities*, when she makes this claim about the prophetic careers of Deborah and Huldah: "Their exercise of their calling must have been at best part-time, at least during child-rearing years, and may not even have begun until later in life. For the Israelite woman such a profession could only have been a second vocation. Early marriage, with its demand upon women of a primary vocation as wife and mother, would have excluded the early cultivation of the gift of prophecy."[16] Unless, of course, these women were never mothers in the first place.

Esther Fuchs, in "Literary Characteristics of Mothers and Sexual Politics in the Hebrew Bible," maintains the biblical emphasis on a woman's value being grounded in motherhood by stating that women are never shown in the biblical stories as being reluctant to give birth much less capable of *not* desiring sons.[17] A contradiction to this point seems to be implicit in several stories and perhaps most clearly in the story of the great woman of Shunem and her encounters with Elisha found in 2 Kgs 4:8–37. While

13. Ackerman, *Warrior, Dancer, Seductress, Queen*, 42.

14. Ackerman, *Warrior, Dancer, Seductress, Queen*, 63.

15. Bronner, *Stories of Biblical Mothers*, 44–45.

16. Bird, *Missing Persons and Mistaken Identities*, 41.

17. Fuchs, "The Literary Characterization of Mothers," 162.

Rachel Haverlock briefly addresses the idea of woman's natural desire for motherhood, in her compelling piece, "The Myth of Birthing the Hero: Heroic Barrenness in the Hebrew Bible," she still concludes, along with Fuchs, that "the procreative context is the only one which allows for a direct communication between woman and YHWH."[18] While the biblical text does not describe the encounters of Huldah or Deborah with God, the text presumes that at least Deborah received a word from the Lord about going into battle against King Jabin's army, and this was done outside of a "procreative" context. "Type-casting" ancient women as mothers "may miss the bigger—and more realistic—picture of women's complex and fluid identities."[19]

A Childfree Feminist Approach

My approach to this topic falls within the broad category of *feminist*, but of course given the diverse definitions and applications of this term, I will try to articulate my understanding of what I mean by a "feminist approach." On a basic level, I subscribe to the definition given by Phyllis Bird in her essay "What Makes a Feminist Reading Feminist: A Qualified Answer," in *Escaping Eden*: "Feminism may be described as a commitment to assert the full humanity of women wherever that is denied, diminished or subordinated to male models."[20] In this book, I offer a critique of the patriarchal constraints placed on women by defining all women solely as a means for producing male heirs and satisfying their desire to preserve immortality through their sons and to feed their patrilineal pride.[21] However, I also seek to do what Pamela Thimmes, in her essay also from *Escaping Eden*, "What Makes a Feminist Reading Feminist: Another Perspective," states is the constructive task of a feminist reading: "advocacy (toward a paradigm of radical equality)."[22] Bird puts it this way: "[Feminism] is thus a political movement for change, grounded in social analysis and drawing on women's experience as the primary source for its critical and constructive work."[23]

---

18. Fuchs, "The Literary Characterization of Mothers," 165. See also Havrelock, "The Myth of Birthing the Hero," 161–62.

19. Gansell, "Women's Lives in the Ancient Near East," 20.

20. Bird, "What Makes a Feminist Reading Feminist?," 124.

21. Cohen, "Why Have Children?," 49.

22. Thimmes, "What Makes a Feminist Reading Feminist?," 135.

23. Bird, "What Makes a Feminist Reading Feminist?," 124–25.

As a biblical scholar, I have placed my feminist commitments at the forefront of researching and writing this book. I read every biblical text, or any text for that matter, with a hermeneutic of suspicion, seeking to see beneath the overt, and implicit, propaganda present in the production of these stories. I seek to study the stories about women as a woman, evaluating the gender constructs at work in their portrayal and asking questions about how the texts conceal and reveal the voices and concerns of both the women from ancient cultures and the women who read them today. I have been influenced by the work of Queer interpretation.[24] In particular, I seek to raise concerns about presuppositions by the biblical writers and audiences and by later interpreters. I draw on the work of Caryn Tamber-Rosenau so that some of the questions behind this research include her own inquiries: "Do the texts presuppose that female characters must be mothers? Are these presuppositions undermined by the same texts that produce them? How are presuppositions about maternity used in the plots of these texts? Do the texts sometimes fail to have their characters perform the relationships to motherhood that we might expect?"[25]

Similar questions can be asked about biblical interpreters and their interpretations of childfree female characters. Do interpreters or readers presuppose that female characters must be mothers, even if the characters are never described as such in the text? Do interpreters or readers exhibit a need to reclaim and expand the concept of mother to entail more than a biological descriptor? Do interpreters or readers speak of characteristics or actions exhibited by female characters (e.g., protection, compassion, and so forth) as rationale for claiming the title of mother for otherwise childfree women? With awareness and release of these interpretive lenses, a different understanding of childfree female characters can emerge that lifts up the roles they fulfill—roles that are completely unrelated to procreation—perhaps even made more feasible by their freedom from motherhood and all of its risks and responsibilities.

In this book, the work of gender theory has shaped my approach in that I attempt to avoid any essentialist notions of womanhood or even motherhood.[26] In fact, behind my work is a basic challenge to patriarchal

24. Certainly, within the world of the Hebrew Bible, being a childfree woman was considered queer.

25. Tamber-Rosenau, "The 'Mothers' Who Were Not," 187. She states her reliance on the work of Ken Stone, specifically his essay "Gender Criticism."

26. Ruane, "When Women are Not Enough," 244–45.

and pronatalist[27] views of women as primarily reproductive avenues for males and for society as a whole. Even females have been formed by these structures so that we too tend to assume the importance of and desire for motherhood for every female. To quote Simone de Beauvoir, "One is not born, but rather becomes, a woman."[28] The question here is how "becoming a woman" is linked to motherhood by both the ancient cultures of the Hebrew Bible and by the contemporary context of the twenty-first-century United States. For many people, the beginning of womanhood is directly related to the onset of a female's menses. In the ancient Near East,[29] this was usually the indication that a female was ready to be "given" to a man as his wife. Similarly, in today's society, the importance of menstruation is that it indicates a female has the biological potential to become pregnant and birth children. While the use of the slang word, "curse,"[30] has been prevalent among women to refer to their cycles, comfort is often offered in reminding the female that she has now reached maturity and can one day fulfill her dream of being a mother. This assumption is certainly prevalent in the Hebrew Bible and is powerfully expressed in Rachel's cry in Gen 30:1: "Give me children or I shall die!" What effect does this assumption have on women who either by circumstance or choice are not mothers? Is a child-free female also a woman, equal to those who do reproduce? Can lifting up such childfree female characters in the stories of the Hebrew Bible provide ways to describe and celebrate women beyond their wombs?

These questions also require some exploration of the historical backdrops for the biblical texts, both Israelite and the broader ancient Near Eastern context. While I do not claim these biblical characters to be actual historical figures, there appearance in stories is the product of the ancient storytellers' and writers' imaginations, which were influenced

27. Pronatalism (also known as natalism or probirth) is a political term. A basic definition would be ". . . an attitude or policy that is pro-birth, that encourages reproduction, that exalts the role of parenthood," Peck and Senderowitz, *Pronatalism*, 2.

28. Beauvoir, *The Second Sex*, 301.

29. The term *ancient Near East* refers to a region that covers the current Middle East, along with Turkey and Egypt. Mesopotamia ("land between the rivers") refers to a portion of the ancient Near East between the Tigris and Euphrates Rivers, essentially what is known today as Iraq. Some of the earliest civilizations arose within Mesopotamia and the ancient Near East.

30. While this may not be common slang for all females, it was certainly prevalent in the shadows of Appalachia where I grew up. I will note briefly the biblical background for using "curse" to describe menstruation, as it reflects a traditional but mistaken interpretation of Gen 3 in which women are "cursed" for "original sin."

by the cultures they experienced. When the gleanings from sociohistorical criticism are paired with literary considerations about genre, setting, characters, and plot, depth and breadth are provided for the texts under consideration. I see this acquired information to provide a foundation for the feminist interpretations provided here.

In this work, I not only presume the biased historical and cultural perspectives of the biblical writers, but I also acknowledge that all interpretation is limited by the specific reading location of the reader or exegete. As Esther Fuchs explains in "Reclaiming the Hebrew Bible for Women," "Feminist epistemology rejects the construction of a monolithic truth, of a position of objectivity, neutrality, and reason, admitting instead to its own partiality as bound by historical context and political perspective."[31] Both the motivation behind the current study and the approach taken are undeniably biased by my own context (my own who, what, when, and where).

Some of the more basic elements of my reading location are that I am an Anglo woman with a PhD, a person educated in a Western context, someone living out of what might be called the socioeconomic middle class of the United States—certainly in a very privileged position within a global context. I am a cisgendered, heterosexual female in a thirty-plus-year marriage, a professor of biblical studies, particularly of the Hebrew Bible, and an ordained minister in a mainline Protestant denomination. I grant the biblical texts some measured amount of authority. There is one other bias that I bring to this research; I am not a mother, because I have chosen not to have children. Thus, the opportunity to reconsider biblical women who are also not defined by being a mother is of great interest and importance to me on a personal level.

In this book I do not claim to speak for all women who are childfree (by circumstance or by choice); rather, I use my experience as a starting point for examining this topic. This study is not intended to disparage the important role of mothers, both in the biblical stories and in today's world, nor to deny the careful consideration that women give to the choice to become a mother. While some of my conclusions could be helpful for women who are struggling with infertility, I recognize that there is absolutely no comparison between being childless due to infertility and being childfree by choice. I do hope to offer an alternative way of seeing women that goes against the deeply entrenched notion that motherhood and womanhood must be synonymous. Perhaps I can provide through this examination of

31. Fuchs, "Reclaiming the Hebrew Bible for Women," 50.

some women in the Hebrew Bible the opportunity for what Mary Gillespie, in "Childfree and Feminine," envisions: an opportunity "for women to shape a fulfilling gender identity that is separate and uncoupled from the hegemonic ideal of motherhood . . . [and] create new possibilities to forge a childfree femininity."[32]

32. Gillespie, "Childfree and Feminine," 134.

2

THE QUEST FOR CHILDFREE WOMEN

Barrenness Everywhere

Beginning in Gen 11, the biblical story presents the first of many barren women. This note about Sarai, wife of Abram, seems to indicate that her barrenness is not a desired status. She is defined by what she lacks: "Now Sarai was barren; she had no child" (Gen 11:30). While this lack would be seen as problematic within an ancient Near Eastern context, it does not seem to have been a cause of great concern for either Abram or Sarai. Given her age (over eighty according to the text's chronology), and the fact that Abram does not seem to have taken a second wife, Sarai's barrenness had not limited her life. In fact, having avoided the inherent risks of pregnancy and childbirth was probably a big contributor to her long life.

The first indication of Sarai's lack of children is found in Gen 15:2, when Abram doubts the Divine promise of progeny because he "will die childless." The next verse indicates that the blame actually lies with the Divine because Abram declares: "Since you have given me no offspring" (15:3). However, as Abram will learn, the Holy keeps covenant and Abram will indeed have offspring. Through trials and tribulations, Sarah does bear Abraham a son, Isaac. Having now fulfilled her "duty," Sarah is portrayed as a protective mother in Gen 21, and her death is recorded in the opening verses of Gen 23. The text provides her age at death (127) and details about where she died.

Thus begins the saga of ancestral barrenness. After Sarah's birthing of Isaac (Gen 21), there is a succession of barren wives. First, Rebekah is said to be barren until her husband, Isaac, prays on her behalf (Gen 25:21). Perhaps the most telling story about the pronatalist pressure upon women to give birth is found in the baby competition that ensues between Rachel and Leah, both wives of Jacob. Leah's pain of not being her husband's favorite is assuaged by the Holy by giving her offspring. However, birthing seven children does not fill this void in her life. On the other hand, Rachel has Jacob's love but still desires to have a child. Despite his devotion, Rachel's desperation to be a mother culminates in her begging Jacob to "give me children, or I shall die!" (Gen 30:1). In this story, the Holy is directly implicated for Rachel's infertility by the statement that "God opened her womb" (Gen 30:22). Of course, Rachel does indeed become a mother to two children. Ironically, given her desperate cry in Gen 30:1, it is her second pregnancy and childbirth that causes her death, due to birthing complications (Gen 35:16–18).

While fertility concerns fade from the story of Exodus, they do arise in later stories. The first is in Judg 13, the beginning of the story about Samson and his exploits. While she is never given a name, Manoah's wife is introduced in the first scene as "barren" and having not "borne any children" (Judg 13:2). When she is visited by an angel, her barrenness is again lifted up in the midst of a birth announcement; her having borne no children is only a temporary condition (13:3). While this woman's barrenness does not seem to be a problem for her, the same cannot be said for Hannah, the next barren woman encountered in the storyline. In the opening chapter of 1 Samuel, Hannah appears as one of the wives of Elkanah. Immediately, a contrast is drawn between Hannah and Peninah (1:3–8); while the latter has given birth to children, Hannah has none. Her status might be seen by society as a negative, but Elkanah favors his first wife and dotes more on her than Peninah and her children. However, Peninah constantly reminds Hannah of her lack in having produced no offspring. This, along with societal pressure, distresses Hannah. When Elkanah makes his next pilgrimage to Shiloh, Hannah accompanies him, and while she is in the sanctuary of Shiloh, her desperation motivates Hannah to deliver a passionate plea for the Holy to give her son. To show her gratitude for such a gift, she promises to dedicate the child to serving the Holy at Shiloh (1 Sam 1:9–11). Hannah's visible expression of distress in her prayer demonstrates the heavy responsibility placed upon women to produce a child. When her prayer is answered (1 Sam 1:20), Hannah's status increases both in her own eyes and in the sight of society. The fact that she dedicates Samuel to the service of the Holy at Shiloh immediately after the child is weaned (1 Sam 1:22–28) seems to indicate that raising a child was not as important as having birthed one. In the Hebrew Bible, motherhood is more about the womb than the woman.

So why all the barrenness and focus on "open" or "closed" wombs? There seem to be at least two possible motivations behind these stories. First, given the precarious nature of life in the ancient Near East, especially in the land where Israel emerged, people were fearful of dying out or being exterminated by a famine, plague, or war. These stories can reflect this preoccupation with death and the future. With the added ingredient of faith in an all-powerful deity, Israel told these stories as a way of proclaiming that despite evidence to the contrary, their god was one who kept covenant by bringing life out of barrenness and providing a future for those who held no hope. Barren women proved the power of the deity over life and death.

Another possible function of these stories about women who had not borne children might have been to prop up the pronatalist ideals of those who told, repeated, collected, or perpetuated the texts. Not only are offspring seen as necessary for survival, but they are also viewed as a means to build up one's power and importance. Israel was never the largest or most powerful nation in the ancient Near East, so a steady increase in population translated into the nation's being a greater power, one that should not be trivialized. However, in order for the primarily male leadership to strong-arm women into bearing as many children as possible, despite the inherent risks involved, there must have been a clear and consistent message that a woman's worth was determined by the fruit of her womb (children in general and sons specifically). The stories that portray the matriarchs of the faith as desperate for motherhood and finding happiness in birthing a child taught females that this was how they should seek happiness in their lives. Connecting infertility with a divine cause provided added pressure, lest a woman be determined as unpleasing to the Holy. Barrenness is suggested as a flaw in character, as a lack of blessing from the Divine. Thus, a woman's sole purpose and ambition should be to produce as many children as possible. As the story of Rachel displays, she is to do this even at risk to her own life. Dying without having given birth to a child meant that she had failed to fulfill the divine purpose for her life and left her with no way to be remembered in the future.

A Case of Forced Motherhood?

Could this emphasis on motherhood have been so strong that women were actually forced into motherhood? One could make this argument about Sarah, who had lived a long life without children, and she and Abraham seemed to accept this situation. Even with the lack of an heir for Abraham, that situation was rectified when Hagar became a surrogate (Gen 16). However, the Divine was not satisfied; the covenant required that Sarai give birth to a child (specifically, a son), no matter what the cost. Those who composed this story may have created the Holy in their image, reflecting their own prejudices and pronatalist ideas. These storytellers insert their own bias that women must give birth in order to be valued by the Divine. Is there any evidence of this heavy-handed approach to women's reproductive abilities?

The story of the Shunammite woman and Elisha (2 Kgs 4:8–37) emerges as a possible example of a childfree woman who was forced into motherhood. The Shunamite woman and her husband do not seem overly concerned about not having a child. If they did, then Elisha's asking the woman how he might repay her for her hospitality would certainly have elicited a request that she be granted a child. Instead, she states very clearly that her life is full, and she does not need the itinerant prophet to grant her a wish. However, the woman's failure to birth a child is seen by Elisha (at the prompting of his servant, Gehazi) as a problem to fix. His promise that she will bear a son "in due time" does not elicit a joyful response, and the experience of motherhood causes her emotional trauma in the illness and death of her child. Could this story of the Shunammite woman and her "forced motherhood" be a glimpse into an area previously uncharted: women in the Hebrew Bible who carefully avoid pregnancy and the requisite role of mother?

Defining Childfree Women

While rare, female characters do appear in the Hebrew Bible without being named as mothers or as barren. They are remembered in the sacred texts for functions unrelated to reproduction. Their presence raises the question of whether motherhood or barrenness were the only two options for women. While they might not have a name ascribed to them, that does not detract from their importance. There are countless mothers and barren women who remain nameless in the Hebrew Bible. Even though this is not the prominent portrayal of women in the biblical texts, their status as child-free is not of concern to the storytellers. Likewise, these females' fulfillment of roles or positions of authority (often ones reserved for males) is not presented as unique or notable. Given that such women are not particularly given narrative asides that point out their noteworthiness, it is possible to consider that the ancient audiences would not have been shocked or confused by these portrayals. In Mesopotamia, we find groups of women who lived outside of matrimony.[1] Perhaps there were many other females who had similar functions and were childfree in their cultures, so imagining women beyond their reproductive function would not be too difficult for the ancient audiences of the Hebrew Bible.

It is important to define what is meant by a *childfree woman*. In the context of the Hebrew Bible, this term applies to female characters who are never described as biological mothers or as barren. Some might suggest that these women did have children, but they are not included in the story. Given the strong emphasis on reproduction and motherhood in the Hebrew Bible, the absence of the word for "mother" and of the name of at least one offspring are irregularities in the texts. In addition, since this approach does not require these women to be historical figures, the concern here is whether they are portrayed as childfree in the biblical story. Since there are no children attributed to them in the world of the biblical story, we can consider them childfree. What is important is that these women play important roles in their narratives, roles that do not include giving birth to a child; they are remembered for fulfilling different roles, some that might surprise biblical readers.

Other Roles for Women in the Ancient Near East

Were there options for women in the ancient Near East for fulfilling, meaningful roles in society that did not involve their own reproductive system? Could women find opportunities for service that did not allow them to have children, or perhaps positions in which being childfree was a requirement? In fact, there is evidence from the cultures surrounding ancient Israel (the culture behind the Hebrew Bible) of women participating in a variety of important roles that one might think only men could fulfill. These women are in positions of authority and hold occupations that are not reliant on

1. Halton and Svärd, trans. and eds., *Women's Writing of Ancient Mesopotamia*,19.

their reproductive abilities. Some professions appear to exclude women with children due to the requirements of the work, including location, time consumption, necessary tasks outside the home, and age.

Finding information about women in ancient cultures is not as easy as it may sound. While the Hebrew Bible provides a biased description of the land known as Israel, Judah, Judea, or Palestine in the period known as the Iron Age (1200–500 BCE), there are other resources that reflect not only the cultures behind the Hebrew Bible but also surrounding cultures prior to and contemporary with ancient Israel.[2] The findings of archeology provide this data, including material remains and written materials; however, these discoveries must be interpreted just like the biblical texts. The history of archeological endeavors reveals some biases that have hindered the study of women in the ancient Near East. One bias is that the majority of both archeologists and directors of archeological digs have been overwhelmingly male, with women's participation being a modern development.[3] While the inclusion of female archeologists does not guarantee a more gender-balanced approach, it certainly seems to put forward a new focus on women in ancient cultures. In addition, the focus on urban centers for digs has resulted in more attention being given to the dominant players in ancient cities, namely men. More recent archeological expeditions in the ancient Near East have sought to overcome these and other biases.

The demands of motherhood in this time period required that women devote all of their time and energy to the tasks necessary for household survival (e.g., food preparation, weaving, pottery, and so forth) and for them to remain in the home for childbearing and childrearing tasks (e.g., breastfeeding and other responsibilities). The inherent risks of pregnancy and childbirth resulted in female deaths at young ages. Carol Meyers has noted that "the mortality rate of females in the child-bearing years greatly exceeded that of the males (Genovés 1969:441–43; Goldstein 1969: 486). In a population in which the life expectancy for men would be 40, women would have a life expectancy closer to 30."[4] It is not impossible to imagine that some women in the ancient society would choose to avoid motherhood given the inherent threats of pregnancy and childbirth. In fact, in various

2. These would include, but not be limited to Sumerian, Akkadian, Hittite, Assyrian, Babylonian, and Persian

3. Nakhai, "Factors Complicating the Reconstruction of Women's Lives." See also Nakhai, "Women in Israelite Religion." Nakhai provides some excellent insights about archeology and women's lives in ancient Israel.

4. Meyers, "The Roots of Restriction," 95.

places in the Hebrew Bible, the image of childbirth is used to describe some national horror to come or already being experienced.[5] Bergmann notes the prevalence of the birth metaphor in the ancient Near East and in the Hebrew Bible to describe times of crisis. "Giving birth became one of the metaphors that helped interpret human history by analogy with the history of a female human being."[6] For contemporary readers, it may be hard to see a connection about impending doom and the birth of a child, which we see as a happy and hopeful event. However, we must see the metaphor in its ancient context. The fact that the image does not include the actual birth but just the experience of childbirth is a first insight into this metaphor and what it can tell us about the dangers inherent in the birthing process for the woman.

In the ancient Near East, the beginning of birth pains did not mean that the survival of the child and mother was assured. There were too many risks. Some archeological evidence suggests that the average woman in ancient Israel had eight pregnancies that were carried to term,[7] not counting the number of miscarriages, many of which may have occurred before the woman knew she was pregnant. As Kalmonofsky states, "The Bible portrays childbirth in terms of feeling vulnerable, for instance, repeatedly mentioning being 'seized' or 'gripped' by labor. By highlighting the vulnerability of a laboring woman, the image connotes weakness and helplessness."[8] For ancient audiences, the parallel drawn between a crisis and a woman giving birth made sense; both were liminal events that had the power to bring death.

Ancient Birth Control Methods

Was being a childfree woman even a possibility for a woman in the ancient Near Eastern context that gave rise to the stories in the Hebrew Bible? While the desire not to reproduce could have been imagined, how would a woman go about preventing conception, other than by abstinence? While

5. For example, Isa. 21:3–4, 23:4, 26:17–18, 42:14, 66:7–8; Mic. 4:9–10; Jer. 4:31, 6:24, 13:21, 22:23, 30:5–6, 48:41, 49:22, 24, 50:43. These texts are identified in Kalmonofsky, "Israel's Baby," 64.

6. Bergmann, *Childbirth as a Metaphor for Crisis*, 218.

7. Bergmann, *Childbirth as a Metaphor for Crisis*, 218. Of those eight pregnancies, an average of two children survived to adulthood.

8. Kalmonofsky, "Israel's Baby," 66.

not a prevalent topic in the Hebrew Bible, the existence of means for birth control is found in extrabiblical literature. Birth control was "a part of folk culture, and women's folklore in particular, in nearly all societies. Even though women rarely had a formal or absolute right to decide unilaterally when to bear children and when not to, women's birth control practice was usually respectable. At other times it was practiced illegally, its technology passed on by an underground of midwives and wise women."[9] Ancient documents from Israel's neighbors even go as far as providing exact descriptions (prescriptions?) for how to prevent, as well as modes of terminating, unwanted pregnancies. This information was often provided by medical practitioners, but it could also have been provided by local healers, perhaps a common knowledge shared among women.

Two plants in particular were understood by ancient cultures to have contraceptive powers: silphium and asafoctida.[10] The demand for silphium as both cough syrup and as a contraceptive may explain how this herb became extinct.[11] Egyptians also had ways to prevent pregnancy, and use of these birth control methods is known as early as 1550 BCE. In the Elders Papyrus are lists of substances ostensibly for ending a pregnancy in even the third trimester, primarily in the form of pessaries. In addition, various concoctions were utilized as blocking agents to prevent pregnancy, including crocodile dung mixed with soured milk and a mixture of acacia leaves, honey, and lint. The effectiveness of these ancient methods is not known, but their continued use at least speaks to a belief in their efficacy.[12] "They are evidence not only of the desire to control reproduction but also of the conviction that it is proper to do so and of the aspiration to do so."[13]

Within the Hebrew Bible, we do have at least one example of a prophylactic practice: "pulling out" or *coitus interruptus*. In Gen 38, the story of Tamar and Judah is told both to explain the existence of two descendants of Judah (Perez and Zerah) and to emphasize the importance of a man having a male heir. In a somewhat awkward portrayal of the so-called levirate marriage custom, Tamar marries Judah's eldest son, Er, who then dies before siring a son. Judah then gives Er's younger brother, Onan, to act as

---

9. Gordon, *The Moral Property of Women*, 13.

10. Riddle et al., "Ever Since Eve," 30.

11. Riddle et al., "Ever Since Eve," 30.

12. Gordon, *The Moral Property of Women*, 19. See also Riddle et al., "Ever Since Eve," 31.

13. Gordon, *The Moral Property of* Women, 14.

Tamar's husband in order to produce a male offspring that would be considered the son of Er. With this set up in which Onan would be supplanted in inheritance if he impregnates Tamar and a son is born, Onan refuses to participate and "spills his seed on the ground" (v. 9). This prophylactic act is judged as unacceptable by the storyteller and the Divine, so Onan is struck dead on the spot. With this kind of lesson story, it would be easy to see why birth control would be a taboo subject for the biblical storytellers, especially with the precariousness of Israel's survival as a people much less a nation. It is left to Tamar to procure an heir for Er and also to guarantee her own security and future by tricking Judah. Only when Tamar bears two boys does the story find a resolution: Er with an heir and Tamar having fulfilled her commanded role as a woman (vv. 12–30). It may be safe to assume that in the cultures behind the Hebrew Bible there were known ways to prevent or to end pregnancy, but they were probably part of female wisdom that did not make it into the biblical texts because of their male authorship and a pronatalist stance.

Examples of Roles for Women in the Ancient Near East

Since storytellers and writers often reflect their own environment, one might wonder if it was even possible the biblical storytellers could've imagined women fulfilling roles in society that did not require them to produce the right offspring. While in the biblical texts most of the roles prominently fulfilled by women involve their reproductive capabilities, outside the biblical texts we have evidence of women in other cultures who held important positions that did not require them to be mothers. In fact, some of these roles fulfilled by women excluded those who were mothers and made it very clear that women in these roles could not bear children themselves. Among occupations we find in other cultures (and in the Hebrew Bible) are cultic personnel, scribes, businesswomen, midwives, and shamans.[14] Warrior and advisory roles within the royal court (roles as wise women) were also available. While not all were unmarried, some of these women were also not married, or at least not living with a male. "The eminent scholar Amélie Kuhrt has convincingly argued that women who had escaped regular masculine authority were considered dangerous for social order and

---

14. Picton, "Living and Working," 239. Picton includes shamans and midwives within the category of wise women.

even possible sources of evil witchcraft."[15] We must keep in mind both the prejudices of ancient authors as well as contemporary ones.

Cultic Personnel

When we speak of cultic personnel, we are primarily speaking of those who would be named priests, either male or female; however, other cultic personnel could also include prophets, diviners, and perhaps even interpreters of religious texts. Among these possible roles, we have evidence of women who were regarded as important cultic figures in the Babylonian dynasty of Hammurabi and his son, dating from 1888 to 1550 BCE. The etymology of the word *naditu*[16] is thought to come from the Akkadian word for "fallow or barren," or "fallow women." Archaeologists have discovered about five hundred texts that give insight into the role of these female functionaries. In her work on the *naditu* women, Harris has suggested that *naditu* women who served the god Marduk could be married but could not bear children.[17] The ones who served the god Shemash could not marry. Another scholar, Jeyes, argues that all *naditu*, regardless of the deity they served, could marry as long as they stayed childfree. There is evidence that these women could acquire for their husbands another wife who would produce an heir for the male. In fact, this was a rather common practice during the Babylonian dynasty. Because these women never dealt with the risks of pregnancy and childbirth, they often lived longer than other women in that time.[18] In their elder years, the *naditu* women would need someone to be their caregivers, a role that would typically be fulfilled by a woman's children. It was fairly

15. Halton and Svärd, trans. and eds., *Women's Writing of Ancient Mesopotamia*, 20. This could explain the strong exhortations against "magic" in the Hebrew Bible and negative interpretations of the medium of Endor (1 Sam 28).

16. The spelling of this word varies from *naditu* to *nadiatu*. In van Wyck, "Prostitute, Nun or 'Man-Woman,'" 117, she offers this important reminder. "The different *nadiātu* groups possess a variety of attributes, depending on the type of group and social-economic circumstances in space and time, together with the hidden choices and motives of the paterfamilias and male family members."

17. Savina Teubal argues that Sarah was actually a *naditu*, thus explaining her lack of offspring and advanced age. The story of Sarah giving Hagar to Abraham as a "surrogate" could reflect this tradition. For a more detailed consideration read Teubal, *Sarah the Priestess*.

18. Van Wyk, "Prostitute, Nun Or 'Man-Woman,'" 116.

common for these women to adopt a servant or a young *naditu*, who would tend to them until their death.

Other types of female cultic personnel or priests (e.g., *entu*, *ishtaritu*, and *qadishtu*) are found in the literature of other ancient Near Eastern cultures.[19] In Sumerian and Akkadian cultures, the *entu* was the "high priestess" and played a major role in the religious practices of their people. One of the best known of these high priestesses was Enheduanna, the daughter of Sargon of Akkad. Her responsibilities included: "to conduct purification rituals, bring sacrifices in certain months, sing cheerful songs, share a bed with the moon god, look after the temple and compose poetry."[20] The second example, *ishtaritu* ("devotee of Ishtar"), "appears to have been a dedicated woman, who was probably also prohibited from bearing children even though she could marry," while the *qadishtu* ("holy or tabooed or set-apart woman") could bear children.[21] In Egypt, women served as priests for both female and male deities. There is "data which show . . . . women served in temples in the company of men. They received equal wages for equal services."[22] All of these females participated in ceremonies and rituals both separate from and alongside male personnel.

Beyond clerical roles, other positions connected to the religious cult included mourners and musicians. Gadotti identifies "professional mourner" as one of three possible cultic roles for females in Mesopotamia. The other two are female priests and magic specialists or diviners.[23] There are clear examples of women fulfilling both roles. "In the ancient Near East and Aegean, professional mourners were almost always women; and in Egypt they were exclusively women."[24] This is true of the Hebrew Bible, where professional mourning women are mentioned in several places (e.g., 1 Samuel, Jeremiah, and Ezekiel). Musicians included both instrumentalists

19. Stuckey, "Priestesses and Sacred Prostitutes," 6.

20. Stol, *Women in the Ancient Near East*, 564. Enheduanna is often proclaimed as the first known poet of the ANE.

21. Stuckey, "Priestesses and Sacred Prostitutes," 7. This word, *qadishtu*, has a parallel in Hebrew, *qedeshah*, which comes from the Hebrew word for "holy." While in the Hebrew Bible the male form of the word is translated as "holy men" who are included among the priests, the feminine form has been interpreted as a "sacred prostitute" without any textual support.

22. Gosline, "Female Priests," 39.

23. Gadotti, "Mesopotamian Women's Cultic Roles," 65.

24. Meyers, "Women's Religious Life," 518. See also in the same collection Gadotti, "Mesopotamian Women's Cultic Roles," 66.

and singers. "Evidence derived from ceramic figurines and biblical passages indicates that women served as singers and musicians in formal and informal religious contexts alike."[25] While both female and male musicians are found throughout the ancient Near East and Mesopotamia; there is one instrument that seems to be reserved for female musicians. This would be the drum.[26] In fact, many scholars argue that the proper understanding of the instrument Miriam and the other women played in Exod 15 was a "hand-held frame-drum" and not the traditional "tambourine."[27] Both in the Hebrew Bible and the surrounding cultures, women played important roles in the rituals of communal worship.

Prophets/Diviners

There is ample evidence of female prophets or diviners in the cultures that surrounded ancient Israel. In Assyria, scholars have discovered evidence of oracles (who provided answers to seekers' questions) and dream interpreters. There was even a type of prophet, a *Selutu*, who was a female devoted to a deity by a ruler.[28] One of the best parallels to the prophets in the Hebrew Bible is found among the texts related to Mari, an important city in Mesopotamia (c 2900–1780 BCE). Archeologists have discovered documents there that describe different types of prophets (both male and female). Some believe it to be the earliest attestation in Mesopotamia of intuitive divination (receiving messages through informal channels). Some of the prophets described in the texts reflect spontaneity and divine inspiration or initiative, consciousness of mission and presentation of prophecies in front of authority figures, and an ecstatic element (using term loosely). All of these characteristics are similar to those of many of the prophets found in the Hebrew Bible.[29]

The broader role of a diviner included a variety of activities, many of which are performed by females. "Mesopotamian women also seem to have played a significant role in the realm of dream interpretation. As such, women's involvement with the sacred and cult went beyond the boundaries

25. Nakhai, "Gender and Archaeology," 519.

26. Paz, *Drums, Women, and Goddesses*, 89.

27. Meyers, "Women with Hand-Drums."

28. Wilson, *Prophecy and Society*, 114.

29. Brenner-Idan, *The Israelite Woman*, 59–60.

normally outlined in the scholarship."[30] In the Hittite culture, we see a connection to "wise women," this time in the role of diviner.[31] Carvalho and Stokl conclude that "ecstatic or charismatic forms of prophecy seem to have been open to women in most societies."[32] In Assyria, women worked together as diviners, dream interpreters, and "exorcists."[33] "The female contribution to different kinds of divine–human communication is of remarkable significance in the history of religion. This may be understood as implying the gender neutrality of the religious agency, but, on the other hand, it also exhibits specific domains where non-males are allowed to transgress the socially sanctioned gender-based boundaries."[34]

Midwives

The importance of reproduction in the ancient Near East and the dangers inherent in pregnancy and childbirth required skilled professionals to advise expectant mothers and assist with childbirth. Midwives were the ones who filled these roles, and they were perhaps the closest thing to an ob-gyn of today. Not only did these women need to have knowledge and skills related to women's reproductive health, but also they had to be trained in religious/magical rituals (e.g., prayers, amulets, incantations, and so forth) performed to ensure a safe birth of a healthy child.[35] Midwives must be available to go to a woman in labor at all hours of the day and night. While it is often claimed that midwives were postmenopausal grandmothers, there is evidence that childfree women were also able to become midwives. Without the responsibility of their children, they could respond on a moment's notice and travel to the pregnant woman's location.

Since there were no midwifery schools at the time, the necessary skills and knowledge would be handed down from one generation to the next. It is not hard to imagine a guild for midwives to gain their training. In the Hebrew Bible, there are few mentions of midwives prior to the establishment of the monarchy (e.g., Gen 35:17; 38:28; and Exod 1), and the names of

30. Gadotti, "Mesopotamian Women's Cultic Roles," 67.

31. Collins, "Women in Hittite Religion," 336.

32. Stökl and Carvalho. *Prophets Male and Female*, 3.

33. May, "Female Scholars in Mesopotamia?," 151.

34. Nissinen, *Ancient Prophecy*, 319.

35. Beckman, "Birth and Motherhood among the Hittites," 321.

only three are known (i.e., Deborah, Shiphrah, and Puah[36]). As midwives, these women are not described as mothers or as barren. Only after Shiphrah and Puah defy the pharaoh's order to kill male babies does the text of Exodus indicate that they became mothers (Exod 1:20–21). The examples of Shiphrah and Puah may reflect the presence of childfree women among midwives. "Finally, midwives were not only health professionals but also religious specialists. As in other ancient Near Eastern cultures and postbiblical tradition, Israelite midwives would have recited appropriate prayers for the wellbeing of the parturient and child and incantations against the evil forces threatening her and the newborn."[37]

Among Israel's neighbors we do find mention of midwives and their functions within those cultures. "The midwife in fact had two roles to perform. The first of course was to deliver the child. In addition, the act of birth had a strong magical-mythological component, and thus the midwife's other function was to recite incantations on behalf of the mother and the newborn."[38] Often these women were cultic figures, as was the case in Babylon, where the aforementioned *naditu* "was seen as some kind of nurse or midwife, with a special skill in saving infants."[39] In his book *Birth in Babylonia and the Bible*, Stol also considers the evidence for religious women who were midwives. In some written archeological records, the *naditu* women were described as the "women who give the womb life by wisdom."[40] Stol comments that in many languages the word for "midwife" has a connection to wisdom and perhaps connects to the idea of a sage or wise woman.[41] "According to Babylonian mythology, for example, goddesses who act as midwives are called 'wise,' which seems to indicate that midwives belong somewhere in the ancient category of 'wise women.'"[42] Stol also reflects on the laywomen who acted as midwives and their importance in not only assisting with the birth of the child but also in their ability to testify to a child's parentage.[43]

---

36. In her essay, "A New Reading of Shiphrah and Puah," Janssen suggests that Shiphrah and Puah were "Israelite prophetesses with significant medio-magical skills," 23.

37. Meyers, "Women's Religious Life," 518.

38. Collins, "Women in Hittite Religion," 336.

39. Lahtinen, *The nadītum as Businesswoman*, 15.

40. Lahtinen, *The nadītum as Businesswoman*, 172.

41. Stol, *Birth in Babylonia and the Bible*, 171.

42. Marsman, *Women in Ugarit and Israel*, 412.

43 Marsman, *Women in Ugarit and Israel*, 173.

Warriors and Military Commanders

While there is little evidence of women on battlefields in the ancient Near East, that does not mean they were not there. Clearly this is the case in the Hebrew Bible, where we have no information about females engaged in war, except for Deborah and (perhaps) Jael. In some cultures around Israel women did serve as soldiers and military commanders. This was especially true in one of the dominant empires of the time, one which Israel would have experienced. Egypt was known for having powerful female leaders. Even though the majority of pharaohs were male, we do have examples of female leaders (e.g., Hatshepsut, Cleopatra, and others). "Royal women undertake military campaigns whilst others are decorated for their active role in conflict. Women were regarded as sufficiently threatening to be listed as 'enemies of the state', and female graves containing weapons are found throughout the three millennia of Egyptian history."[44] During the ninth century BCE, in Assyria,[45] we have one named female ruler, who also may have engaged in battle. Sammu-Ramat (also known as Semiramis) "took the extraordinary step of accompanying her husband on at least one military campaign, and she is prominently mentioned in royal inscriptions."[46] Upon her husband's death, Sammu-Ramat may have led these military efforts.[47] Later, in sixth-century-BCE Persia, Artunis was a commander in the army of Cyrus the Great. Though little is known about her accomplishments, surely she was not the only female in the Persian military. In fact, archeologists have found "examples of grave goods from excavated tombs which provide ample evidence of women warriors in the Persian army including one woman's tomb from the Achaemenid Period containing a javelin, spear, bow and arrows, and a knife which were clearly her own."[48]

This lack of evidence for females engaged in war does not seem to be due to an ancient perception that women were not violent. One of the most influential deities in the ancient Near East was Anat, who was known as the god of war and hunting. The violence attributed to Anat primarily in Ugaritic text is extreme. She is described as slaughtering her enemies

44. Fletcher, "From Warrior Women to Female Pharaohs."

45. The Assyrians successfully conquered the Northern Kingdom of Israel and put intense pressure on the Southern Kingdom of Judah in the last of the eighth century BCE.

46. Bertman, *Handbook to Life in Ancient Mesopotamia*, 102.

47. Mark "Sammu-Ramat and Semiramis."

48. Mark, "Twelve Great Women of Ancient Persia."

in a "blood bath." "Whatever the impulses and motives behind Anat's acts and threats of violence, there is no denying that this was a major component of her personality."[49] Likewise, Innana/Ishtar is described in Sumerian and Babylonian texts as ferocious and one to be feared for her devastating strength.[50] In an Akkadian composition, Ishtar is portrayed as "a fierce goddess who whirls around in her 'manliness,' whose feast is battle, who goes out in war."[51] Even those who attempt to identify every female deity as a "fertility mother goddess" cannot make Anat and Innana/Ishtar fit into those essentialist categories. The same is true of at least Deborah and Jael in the biblical texts. They refuse to be "motherized" in order not to disturb biblical and contemporary ideas of womanhood.

Scribes and Messengers

In the ancient world, before phones, faxes, telegrams, email, and other contemporary communication technology, the only means of communication between two parties happened via human messengers, often with written documents from the sender. "A correspondent achieved two desirable results when employing simultaneously a messenger and a written letter: 1) precision of the written text and 2) explication of the text through the messenger."[52] Thus, the person sent as messenger would need to be trusted by the sender and capable of not only making the trip but also comfortable in a variety of cultural contexts. Often, female messengers were sent on their errands by women, while men typically utilized male messengers. This is the case for the aforementioned *naditu* women, who were themselves conductors of commerce and who utilized female messengers. In the Hebrew Bible, there is a story that flips that typical equation. David, on the run from Absalom, owes his success to an anonymous "maid" who delivers an important message from Jerusalem (2 Sam 17:17). It is also possible that the plural noun "messengers," when it appears, could have included females, since the masculine plural form of a noun can also refer to a group of men and women. The prophet Isaiah of the exile identifies Zion as female and then describes her as being the messenger of the Holy (Isa 40:9).

---

49. Wilson, "Anat: Autonomous Goddess of Ugarit."

50. Frymer-Kensky, *In the Wake of the Goddesses,* 66.

51. Frymer-Kensky, *In the Wake of the Goddesses,* 67.

52. Meier, "Women and Communication in the Ancient Near East," 540.

If the messenger wrote or read the correspondence (or both), then the role of scribe was also present. "Female literacy and numeracy in Mesopotamia, especially in the early periods, is well known, and the existence of female scribes in most periods of Mesopotamian history is beyond any doubt."[53] While the majority of messenger-scribes attested to in the texts of the ancient Near East are male, there is consistent and substantial evidence that females also fulfilled this role. According to one accounting, there are documents attesting to at least twenty-nine female scribes at work in Mesopotamia.[54] This does not include the other possible females during the time before gendered nouns appear in the writings. Even on a divine level, writing has a feminine element. In Egypt, the deity associated with the invention of writing was the female Seshat. Similarly, in Mesopotamia, the scribal deity is also female, Nisaba, who is later replaced or paired with a male deity Nabu.[55]

A prominent conclusion regarding ancient Israel is that only males were granted the privilege of education. The presence of females who could read, write, or both, throughout the ancient Near East makes such a claim worthy of reconsideration. There is only one clear reference to a female scribe in the Hebrew Bible (Ezra 2:55: *ha'soferet*, which translates as "the scribe" and is a feminine noun but is often rendered incorrectly as a proper noun), but that does not mean that she was the only one in all of Israel's history. If Huldah was able to discern that the scroll found in the temple was authentic (see 2 Kgs 22:8–20), she must have been literate. It is interesting to note that the key figure of wisdom in the Hebrew Bible is woman wisdom of Proverbs. Given the references in the text to Her gathering students and the importance of education within Proverbs, it would be fair to say that woman wisdom was the "the divine patroness of the Israelite school system."[56] Given this strong influence of the feminine within education, it is not a stretch to accept that Israelite women were also allowed an education, though perhaps less often than men and only if they came from wealthy families.

53. May, "Female Scholars in Mesopotamia?," 150.

54. Meier, "Women and Communication in the Ancient Near East," 542.

55. Meier, "Women and Communication in the Ancient Near East," 543.

56. Meier, "Women and Communication in the Ancient Near East," 543. Meier is referencing the work of Bernhard Lang, *Wisdom and the Book of Proverbs*.

Conclusions

This brief consideration of the roles women played within the cultures of the ancient Near East allows us to broaden our perspective on the portrayal of female characters in the Hebrew Bible. When traditional descriptions of exclusively male positions are expanded to include other activities beyond the official ones, we find texts that describe women performing acts that align with the ancient Near Eastern evidence of female cultic personnel, female prophets or diviners, female midwives and physicians, female warriors, and female scribes and messengers. Within the Hebrew Bible, females are portrayed as doing work that extends beyond the household and perhaps requires a certain freedom that childfree women enjoyed. In her book *Women at Work in the Deuteronomistic History*, Bachmann identifies "twenty-five feminine nouns or participles denoting what we would call professions or occupations."[57] While some of the work may have been specific to females, other professions were fulfilled by both females and males. "These terms attest to the variety of tasks women assumed, besides their daily household chores. And one may also imagine there were many others not attested in the sources available to us."[58] I would challenge Bachmann's assertion that all women had "household chores" as their primary responsibility before any other occupation, which seems to indicate her assumption of motherhood for all females.[59]

Mwendambio further delineates the religious activities of female characters in the Hebrew Bible. "They exercised prophetic roles (Exod 15:20; Judg 4:4; Isa 8:3; 2 Kgs 22:14; Neh 6:14), presented gifts for the construction of the tabernacle (Exod 35:20–29), participated in religious processional dance (Ps 68:25), played musical instruments and sang in the temple (1 Chr 25:5–7; Ezra 2:65; Neh 7:67), served at the entrance to the tent of meeting (Exod 38:8; 1 Sam 2:22), celebrated the Passover (Exod 12:43–51), and so forth."[60] Meyers points out that women's participation in communal worship required expertise attained through specialized education and

---

57. García Bachmann, *Women at Work*, 8.

58. García Bachmann, *Women at Work*, 8.

59. Later in her book, she also "motherizes" two childfree female characters. "One should not dismiss female prophetic participation too easily, since the ancestors of prophecy are *two mothers* (italics added), Miriam and Deborah, and both are highly honored in their leading role as singers and musicians, like these prophets" (García Bachmann, *Women at Work*, 174).

60. Mwendambio, "Depiction of the Status of Women," 21.

training. "Divinatory techniques, laments, midwifery incantations, temple music, and the rest involved the acquisition of skill sets or knowledge that served religious purposes . . . And all the practitioners of these skills, perceived as necessary for certain aspects of community life, likewise garnered a measure of prestige."[61] As in other cultures, it is possible that some of these roles emerged as possibilities because the women were free from the obligations of marriage, motherhood, or both.

The women considered in this study are all characters in the narratives of the Hebrew Bible. They are major players in the metanarrative of the faith journey of the people known as Israelites. Whether or not these women are actual historical figures is not relevant to this project. As with many literary characters, these women may represent the roles of women within the cultures that produced the texts. Of particular importance will be our consideration of the variety of roles in which they are portrayed and the common denominator that all of them are childfree.

61. Meyers, "Women's Religious Life," 520.

3

MIRIAM

Worship Leader, Prophet, and Source of Life

Introducing Miriam

Miriam appears as a named character in five biblical texts: Exod 15:20–21 in her role as worship and song leader after the safe crossing of the Sea of Reeds; Num 12 in the story of her (and perhaps Aaron's) challenge of Moses' authority as God's only prophet (later referenced in Deut 24:9); Num 20:1 where her death is recorded; Num 26:59, where she is named as one of Jochebed's three children (duplicated in 1 Chr 6:3); and Mic 6:4, where the prophet identifies her as one of the three liberators that God called to lead the Israelites out of Egypt. While no name is given in Exod 2:1–9 for the sister who plays a vital role in the story of the infant Moses' survival, the text in Num 26:59 would seem to support that this had to be Miriam, since Jochebed is not described as having any other daughters.

Despite the blatant lack of evidence that Miriam was married or was a mother, scholars still place her within so-called metaphorical motherhood. In her essay, "'Mother in Israel': A Familiar Figure Reconsidered," J. Cheryl Exum writes, "the exodus has three figurative mothers as well: Shiphrah and Puah, the midwives who defy Pharaoh's command to kill male Hebrew babies, and Moses' sister, whose resourcefulness at a strategic moment determines Moses' future and who later becomes a leader of the exodus in her own right."[1] In her interpretation of Num 20, Dvora Lederman-Daniely describes Miriam as "the symbol of femaleness—representing the intensities of birth, nourishing and preserving life."[2]

While the sister in Exod 2 fulfills a protective role often attributed to mothers but also could be the action of big sisters, there is no evidence that Miriam displays such maternal behavior toward Moses (or Aaron) in her other appearances in the biblical story. In fact, the opposite could be said in the case of her confrontation with Moses (Num 12), and her song at the crossing of the sea (Exod 15:20–21) shows no acknowledgment of her brother's lengthier celebration of the people's safety (Exod 15:1–18). The texts portray her as a leader of her people, often contesting Moses' solo approach to leadership, and as a prominent person in the exodus saga. Her childfree status does not seem to be problematic for the biblical storytellers, and perhaps it gave her the freedom to do the tasks Miriam was called to accomplish.

Miriam as Prophet and Worship Leader—Exodus 15:20–21

> 20Then the prophet Miriam, Aaron's sister, took a tambourine in her hand; and all the women went out after her with tambourines and with dancing. 21 And Miriam sang to them: "Sing to the Lord, for the Lord has triumphed gloriously; horse and rider the Lord has thrown into the sea." [NRSV, alt]

Miriam's first named appearance in the biblical text is Exod 15:20–21. When the Israelites successfully cross the sea and the Pharaoh's army is swallowed up by the waters, the text describes Moses singing a song celebrating God's victory (Exod 15:1–18). The words of this long and elaborate hymn are attributed to Moses as a solo performance. There are questions about the origins and authorship of this part of the chapter. Some have argued that Moses' song (or at least part of it) seems to come from a later time period because it includes images of God's leading the people through the wilderness and of the settlement in the promised land. Others have argued that

---

1. Exum, "'Mother in Israel,'" 80. While Exum is trying to speak of the important roles women play in the Hebrew Bible, she still defines them as "mothers"—whether biological or "figurative." Why try to force Miriam, and others, into the mold of motherhood when their importance in the story has absolutely nothing to do with their reproductive organs?

2. Lederman-Daniely, "Revealing Miriam's Prophecy," 25.

the words of his song were originally attributed to Miriam, who also sings a victory song.[3]

After the conclusion of Moses' song is an introductory line, stating again that the sea had drowned the Egyptian army but permitted the Israelites to cross on dry ground. This is followed by the statement that Miriam took a drum and led the women in song and dance. Her brief hymn is recorded in v 21: "Sing to the Lord, for the Lord has triumphed gloriously; horse and rider the Lord has thrown into the sea." In fewer than ten words, Miriam summarizes what it takes Moses ten verses to do. Some scholars suggest that Exod 15:1–21 has been edited so that words have been rearranged, and that Moses's voice (rather than Miriam's) has been made primary.[4]

In explaining the redaction of the text, J. Gerald Janzen argues that the Song of Miriam should come after 15:8, thus making the song of Moses a response to her words. It is Miriam who leads the whole community in a song of celebration in response to the Divine's acting on their behalf. "If 15:19–21 is indeed an analepsis, positioning us at 14:29, then the people's response in 14:31, and especially in 15:1–18, suggests that it is the people as a whole to whom Miriam sings and whom she bids sing."[5] Cross and Freedman, however, make the case that the entire twenty-one verses should be attributed to Miriam. They state that "vs. 21 is not a different or shorter or the original version of the song, but simply the title of the poem taken from a different cycle of traditions."[6] While it can be easily explained how later traditions came to associate the hymn with the renowned prophet Moses, it is more difficult to imagine that Miriam would have been added at a later point.[7] Another piece of evidence to support Miriam's being the author of the entire hymn is that the Hebrew Bible associates the singing of songs after a military victory to women (e.g., Jepthah's daughter in Judg 11, Deborah and Barak in Judg 5). Thus, it would be the norm for Miriam and the other women to sing and dance after the miraculous victory at the sea, where the Divine defeated the oppressive empire of Pharaoh.

3. For the dating of the song see Haupt, "Moses' Song of Triumph," 153–54; for Miriam as original author, see Cross and Freedman, "The Song of Miriam," along with Janzen, "Song of Moses, Song of Miriam."

4. See Janzen, "Song of Moses, Song of Miriam"; and Kamionkowski, "Will the Real Miriam Please Stand Up?"

5. Janzen, "Song of Moses, Song of Miriam," 215–16.

6. Cross and Freedman, "The Song of Miriam," 237.

7. Cross and Freedman, "The Song of Miriam," 237.

It is very possible that a later patriarchal and pro-Moses redactor attempted to downplay the importance of Miriam and emphasize the importance of her brother. As Fokkelien van Dijk-Hemmes and Brenner have stated, the biblical texts were processed through patriarchal views and structures that severely limited and at times erased women's roles and voices from the stories.[8] In a male-dominated traditioning of the materials, it is possible that Exod 15 has been redacted so that Moses is portrayed as the clear leader of the exodus, and Miriam is reduced to a choir director. "In other words, tradition stole Miriam's song and gave it to Moses!"[9]

Given that there is no way to prove conclusively to whom the words of Exod 15:1–18 belong, there is evidence about Miriam that can be gleaned from the verses attributed to her within the text. A close reading of v. 21, though, expands the picture of Miriam's worship leadership. The text states that Miriam took a tambourine, and "all the women went out after her" taking their musical instruments and dancing (Exod 15:20b). This description leaves the readers with an image of Miriam as a worship leader of only the women. Thus, the argument has been made that Miriam was not a leader for the whole community; her leadership was restricted to the women. Some have even used this text to argue against female leadership in worship. However, the imperative verb used in v. 21 ("sing") is a second-person masculine plural form. If Miriam were simply leading an all-female group, this verb should be a second-person feminine plural. The unexpected masculine form is a clue that has been overlooked. In Hebrew, a feminine verb form is used when a group is made up of only females. If the subjects of the verb are male, then the masculine form is employed. The other use for a masculine verb form is when the subjects are a group of women and men. Miriam's command to "sing" was directed at the whole group, males and females. She was recognized as a leader of the gathered community. Even more, her leadership seems to be very different in style from her brother's. While Moses sang a solo, Miriam involved the broader community in her celebration.

As was mentioned above, the story portrays Miriam and the women in the expected roles of celebrating a military victory through music and dance. It would be easy to dismiss this female role as simply a way of welcoming home their warriors (e.g., after the victories of Saul and David in

---

8. Lederman-Daniely, "Revealing Miriam's Prophecy," 10. Lederman-Daniely cites Brenner(-Idan) and Dijk-Hemmes, *On Gendering Texts*, 5–8.

9. Kamionkowski, "Will the Real Miriam Please Stand Up?"

1 Sam 18) and to see the women's involvement as merely a wartime cultural practice. However, some scholars have described these activities as religious rites, "ritual re-enactments of the battle . . . a common practice in Mesopotamian worship."[10] Just as Egyptian women acted as priestesses in this musical procession, it is possible that Miriam is taking a similar role in Exod 15. Given her association with Aaron at the introduction to her song and the ancient context for her hymn, this text seems to indicate that Miriam was a cultic leader in the earliest traditions about Israel's deliverance.

This consideration of Miriam in her first named appearance has not yet considered the question of why she is described in Exod 15:20 as a "prophet." In fact, many have wondered what she does that should be considered "prophetic." If one's definition of *prophet* is based in the idea of foretelling the future, then such a question is understandable. However, Israel's prophets were not primarily concerned with predicting events yet to happen, but they focused their words and actions on their current context. In the words of Abraham Heschel, "prophets gave an exegesis of existence from a Divine perspective."[11] They spoke so that people could change and get back to living in covenantal relationship with the Holy, themselves, and their neighbors. "She is a prophet not because she foresees the future, whatever that may mean. She is a prophet because she sees what, and as, God sees: through the eyes of the oppressed, the despised, the outcasts, the ravaged, the powerless and those who suffer."[12]

The essential task of a prophet was to tell the people what they needed to hear, even when it was not what the people wanted to hear.[13] Miriam's song and actions meet both of these criteria: they explain what happened at the *yam suf* from a divine perspective, and they assure the people that their God sides with the oppressed over and against the oppressor. "Her prophecy, as was perceived by the people, was direct, dialogical and unmediated by ecstatic techniques, trances, etc." Her song was every bit as "authentic" as that of her brother.

10. Kamionkowski, "Will the Real Miriam Please Stand Up?" Egyptian women, specifically, are portrayed as using percussion instruments, thus strengthening the parallel with Miriam and the Israelite women.

11. Heschel, *The Prophets*, xxvii.

12. Boesak, "The Riverbank, the Seashore and the Wilderness," 14.

13. This is the author's own definition of a "prophet."

Miriam as Challenger of Authority—Numbers 12

1 While they were at Hazeroth, Miriam and Aaron spoke against Moses because of the Cushite woman whom he had married (for he had indeed married a Cushite woman); 2 and they said, "Has the LORD spoken only through Moses? Has the LORD not spoken through us also?" And the LORD heard it. 3 Now the man Moses was very humble, more so than anyone else on the face of the earth. 4 Suddenly the LORD said to Moses, Aaron, and Miriam, "Come out, you three, to the tent of meeting." So the three of them came out. 5 Then the Lord came down in a pillar of cloud, and stood at the entrance of the tent, and called Aaron and Miriam; and they both came forward. 6 And the Lord said, "Hear my words: When there are prophets among you, I the LORD make myself known to them in visions; I speak to them in dreams. 7 Not so with my servant Moses; he is entrusted with all my house. 8 With him I speak face to face—clearly, not in riddles; and he beholds the form of the LORD. Why then were you not afraid to speak against my servant Moses?" 9 And the anger of the LORD was kindled against them, and the LORD departed. 10 When the cloud went away from over the tent, Miriam had become leprous, as white as snow. And Aaron turned towards Miriam and saw that she was leprous. 11 Then Aaron said to Moses, "Oh, my lord, do not punish us for a sin that we have so foolishly committed. 12 Do not let her be like one stillborn, whose flesh is half consumed when it comes out of its mother's womb." 13 And Moses cried to the LORD, "O God, please heal her." 14 But the LORD said to Moses, "If her father had but spit in her face, would she not bear her shame for seven days? Let her be shut out of the camp for seven days, and after that she may be brought in again." 15 So Miriam was shut out of the camp for seven days; and the people did not set out on the march until Miriam had been brought in again. 16 After that the people set out from Hazeroth, and camped in the wilderness of Paran.

Miriam's second appearance is in Num 12, where she and Aaron are portrayed as challenging Moses' prophetic authority. While the pretext for their complaint seems to have something to do with Moses' "Cushite" wife, many scholars have suggested that the real issue is something much deeper, summarized in the question, "Has the LORD spoken only through Moses? Has the Holy not spoken through us also?" (Num 12:2 [NRSV, alt]). On the surface, the response seems to be a straightforward confirmation that only Moses, not Miriam or Aaron, is the Lord's prophet (Num 12:3–9). Particularly, Miriam should be punished for her insubordination in daring to criticize Moses much less suggest that she is equivalent to him in prophetic stature (Num 12:10–15). The Divine has spoken—case closed. But what about Aaron? How does he escape punishment for his part in the sedition? How does one reconcile this scene with the labeling of Miriam as a "prophet" in Exod 15 and the later inclusion of her in the prophet Micah's statement about the Holy's triumvirate leaders of the Israelites' liberation? In considering this passage, it is important to remember that the written divine voice in any biblical text should be read with great suspicion, and in this case it is important to ask how has "the word of God [been] recruited and used in political manipulations between power groups"?[14]

If, as some scholars have argued, this scene is really about a power struggle between different groups who are vying for their rightful place of power, a close textual reading of the Hebrew in v. 1 presents an interesting aspect to this story. The verb, translated as a third-person masculine plural verb with both Miriam and Aaron as its subject, appears as a third-person feminine singular form. This has led to the hypothesis that in an original form of this story, Miriam was the only one who challenged Moses, with Aaron being edited into the text later by those attempting to argue against the validity of the Aaronic priesthood. If this is true, then that could explain the rest of the story. God is portrayed as enraged by this questioning of Moses' authority and speaks clearly that Moses is God's chosen prophet, above anyone else. As punishment for this act of sedition, God afflicts Miriam with leprosy; Aaron survives unscathed. But where does this leave Miriam? Was she also seen as a threat to Moses's authority, and by association, to an all-male power structure?

What is Miriam's true concern? Is she really angry about Moses's taking a second wife who is a foreigner (Num 12:1)? Or is this a complaint about Zipporah, his Midianite wife, and the threat that Miriam perceives in her sister-in-law's leadership role? Many scholars have concluded that the term "Cushite" is meant neither as a prejudicial racial comment nor as implying that Moses has married another wife, given the lack of any evidence in the text for his having taken a second wife. If we remember the story found in Exod 4:24–25, where Zipporah performs an emergency circumcision to save (presumably) Moses' life, there might be a suggestion of Miriam's first complaint. Perhaps Miriam sees Zipporah's priestly actions as in competition with her own, as a rival to her position of religious

14. Lederman-Daniely, "Revealing Miriam's Prophecy," 9.

leadership. She thinks that Moses needed to recognize her leadership as being primary to Zipporah's.

The second complaint, about who is or is not a prophet (Num 12:2), a recipient of the divine word, seems to cut closer to Miriam's place within the Israelite community and her recognition as a messenger of the Holy. Given the lack of any information about Miriam having a husband or a family, there would appear to be no reason why she is not able to fulfill this divine calling. Freed from the usual limitations inherent in motherhood of the time period, Miriam has dedicated her life to the service of the Holy and the Holy's people. Perhaps the story of Miriam inspired other women, later in Israel's story, to demand equal leadership in the priesthood and prophetic guilds. From this perspective, when Miriam uses the pronoun "us"(Num 12:2), she is also representing the voices of other women who have followed in her path. If a possible restriction to such female participation was the obligations placed on her as a wife and mother, the tradition of Miriam would be seen as a strong case for women eschewing these traditional roles and seeking the places of power that men were trying to reserve for themselves. Not only would these ideas be seen as threatening the male establishment, but they would also be a direct rebellion against the pronatalist ideology of the nation. There needed to be a story that would remind women of the importance of reproduction, and Num 12 not only provides that message but adds the threatening power of how these women will be dealt with by the Holy. Step out of line, and you will be removed from any place within your community. You will be "as one dead, who emerges from his mother's womb with half his flesh eaten away" (Num 12:12). Although you may live to tell about your experience, you will wish you were dead.

Whatever the cause of the dispute and following punishment of Miriam, the conclusion of the story reveals Miriam's importance in the story of the Israelites. While she is shut out of the community for seven days, the people refuse to move until she can rejoin them (Num 12:15). No matter how hard the male-dominated powers that be tried to silence Miriam and kill her influence within the community, she, and her story, survived. She was a revered and valued leader in the people's eyes. Miriam was the people's prophet. Her presence was seen as vital for their safe passage through the unknown of the wilderness.

Miriam as Source of Life for the People—Numbers 20:1

1 The Israelites, the whole congregation, came into the wilderness of Zin in the first month, and the people stayed in Kadesh. Miriam died there, and was buried there. 2 Now there was no water for the congregation; so they gathered together against Moses and against Aaron.

In the Hebrew Bible, it is quite common to read about the deaths of male characters (e.g., Abraham, Isaac, Jacob, and so forth), and to read information about their age and the place where they died. However, it is less likely to find this information about the passing of female characters. While we do find information about the death of Sarah (Gen 23—age and burial place) and Rachel (Gen 35:16–20—burial place), these are just a handful of exceptions. Thus, when the text provides information about Miriam's death and the place of her final resting, it is important to take note. There is no age given, but the people's loss of their prophet is experienced as a devastating and threatening event.

First, the location of Miriam's burial is important to note. As is often the case, the Hebrew name of a place indicates more than simply its listing on a map. Here, *kadesh* is the word most often translated in reference to holiness or being set aside for a purpose. Why would the storytellers associate Miriam's death with the root word "holy"? Is this an implicit clue to her status as a religious leader a piece of Miriam's tradition that could not be erased from the communal memory by androcentric editors? Perhaps this is a countertradition to the meaning of her leprosy in Num 12. While this skin condition was meant to portray her as ritually impure, in the final word on her life, Miriam is declared *Kadesh*, "holy."

Not only does the story provide the detail of Miriam's death and burial, but the context of these statements is equally important. Immediately following her death notice, the text simply states that the people have no water. Given the absolute necessity of water for survival in the arid climate of the ancient Near East, this association of the loss of life support with the death of Miriam seems intentional. Without their trusted leader, the people now face a struggle to survive. In Miriam's absence, they demand more from Moses and Aaron. Without Miriam, they turn against the remaining male leaders, who seem at a loss as to how to meet the people's needs. Only by divine rescue are Moses and Aaron able to supply what is lacking. Miriam's absence makes appeasing the community's demands as difficult as getting water from a rock.

It is also important to note that this communal threat, a lack of water, leads ultimately to Moses's rash actions of striking the rock (Num 20:11). This very impulsive behavior is what, according to the text, denies Moses entry into the promised land (Num 20:12). The golden calf incident excludes Aaron from this reward (Exod 32). However, Miriam's death is not a punishment for anything she did. It is described as simply part of the circle of life. Although she did not live to see the land flowing with milk and honey, there is no declaration that this was a Divine sentence. Miriam finds eternal rest in a holy place.

Miriam as Liberator—Micah 6:4

> 4 For I brought you up from the land of Egypt, and redeemed you from the house of slavery; and I sent before you Moses, Aaron, and Miriam.

The prophet Micah is usually dated to the eighth century BCE, having been sent to speak a word from the Lord to the people of Jerusalem. The Southern Kingdom of Judah is experiencing a time of peace and prosperity, and nowhere is this more evident than in the capital city of Jerusalem. However, the economic gains are not enjoyed by everyone. The rich are getting richer, while the poor are getting poorer. The powerful believe that their lavish worship will keep the Holy appeased and divert the Divine attention from how they are abusing the oppressed and vulnerable in their community. Micah reminds them that no matter how impressive one's worship service might be, God is unimpressed if worship is not coupled with a concern for the powerless, for the "least of these."

In the midst of the most well known text in Micah, we find Miriam identified as one of the leaders sent by the Holy to bring the Israelites from oppression to freedom. While most usually skip over this part of the pericope in order to focus on Mic 6:8, it is significant that the prophet includes Miriam as part of the divinely chosen freedom trio remembered as heroes of the exodus. Despite efforts by later editors to erase or downplay her leadership, by the time of Micah (or more accurately, when these words were recorded), her memory tenaciously lingered. While other female biblical characters are remembered for birthing the right heir for their husbands, Miriam's stature in the biblical story is not connected to her reproductive abilities but to her strengths as liberator of the people of Israel.

Miriam—A Childfree Woman

If we stay simply with the texts in which Miriam is named, we are given a portrait of a prophet, a musician-priest, and a liberator, like her brothers Aaron and Moses—an important leader of the people. Certainly, the role Miriam fulfills is not the stereotypical one of a prophet: she does not condemn the injustices of her people (though some questions have been raised about what she was protesting in Num 12) or speak of any future punishment for Israel's unfaithfulness. Miriam expands our understanding of a prophet as one who leads the people in naming and celebrating God's presence in their lives. The last we hear about Miriam is that she died and was buried at Kadesh, a place that would later become a holy site for the Israelites. "She [Miriam] serves as a reminder that even in cultures that emphasize domestic roles for women, some women do achieve public leadership."[15] In all of these texts, Miriam is never described as a wife or a mother much less as barren. Is there a reason? Would she have been able to lead the people in worship if she had children to tend to or a spouse to support? Did her being childless or childfree give her the freedom to fulfill her calling from the Holy as a prophet and religious leader?

If, as Num 12 seems to make clear, Moses is God's prophet, and Aaron was chosen to be Moses's prophet, perhaps Miriam was the people's prophet. Despite the fact that the Hebrew Bible describes Miriam as dying unmarried and without children, some later commentators (particularly rabbinic writers), showing their own bias about what makes a woman valuable, suggested that she did marry and give birth to children; thus they remade her into the comfortable idea of a mother.[16] However, based on the biblical texts, Miriam defies this desire to domesticate her character. She refuses to fit within the pronatalist views of the text, and even those of contemporary readers, that base a woman's worth on the fruit of her womb. Miriam was not a so-called mother figure to her brothers or for the people; she was a trusted religious leader and voice for the Holy. Her memory is maintained because of what she could do, without having to be a mother and wife.

15. Sakenfeld, "Numbers," 55.

16. Rabbinic tradition has Miriam as the wife of Caleb; however, the names of Caleb's wives are provided in 1 Chr 2:18–19 as Azubah and Ephrath. See Meir, "Miriam: Midrash and Aggadah."

I am Miriam . . .

I have no call story, . . . yet I am called a prophet.

I am not identified as a priest, . . . yet I am of a priestly lineage and led a religious ritual.

I am chastised for seeking equality, . . . yet the people would not continue without me.

I was buried at a place called Holy/Kadesh, . . . yet you don't know my age.

I was silenced by androcentric interpretations, . . . yet Micah names me among the liberators

My story is incomplete, . . . yet I am not forgotten.

Works so hard to prove & has no children

4

DEBORAH

Judge, Prophet, Warrior, and Poet-Singer

Introducing Deborah

The story of Deborah is found in Judg 4 and 5, in a prose version and in a poem respectively. She is first introduced as a judge and a prophet (Judg 4:4) to whom the Israelites would go for adjudication of their disputes. Later, the texts reveal that Deborah is also a military commander (giving orders to Barak), a warrior (going into battle with the Israelites), and a poet, singer, or both (as primary voice behind the victory song in Judg 5). Within the book of Judges, Deborah is the first one of the judges to be presented by a lengthy introduction. J. Cheryl Exum points to "Deborah as one of the few unsullied leaders"[1] during this time before the monarchy. Some of the male judges that follow are anything but outstanding examples of leadership and faithfulness (e.g., Jephthah [Judg 11] and Samson [Judg 13–16]).

Despite her distinguished career, biblical commentators have attempted to downplay her leadership, claiming she was not a true judge because God had not raised her up (cf. Judg 2:16, 18; 3:9, 15), and that she was not a military hero like the others who bear the title judge in this biblical book.[2]

1. Exum, "'Mother in Israel,'" 84.

2. See for example Block, "The Period of the Judges," 49; Brettler, *The Book of*

43

This diminishing of Deborah is first found in other biblical texts. It is Barak whose name appears on the list of judges found in 1 Sam 12:11, and in the Christian Scriptures, the book of Hebrews replaces Deborah with Barak in the list of the faithful persons in Israel's story (11:32). However, such attempts to discredit her resumé are without merit. As for the lack of the expected element of God "raising up" a leader to save the people, such an accusation could also be made of Jephthah, who was chosen by the frightened people and not originally called to service by the Holy. In responding to this apparent disqualifier of Deborah as judge, Ronald Pierce writes that because "she is the only judge apart from Samuel already in prophetic service before she acts as judge . . . may be the reason she is not described like other judges as being 'raised-up' on a particular occasion."[3] The claim that she lacks military heroism seems to be contradicted by Judg 5:15a, which states that "the chiefs of Issachar followed Deborah"; this is in synonymous parallel relationship with the next line, "and Issachar faithful to Barak" (v. 15a). Clearly, Deborah is portrayed as "the leading human agent of military deliverance"[4] with Barak following her into battle.

More disturbing though is the insistence of scholars to restrict Deborah's role in the story to that of wife and mother. Both male and female scholars seem determined to label her with these more traditional roles of women. In her essay, "'I Arose a Mother in Israel': Motherhood as Liberating Power in the Biblical Stories of Miriam and Deborah," Dvora Lederman-Daniely insists on labeling Deborah (along with Miriam) as a mother, despite her having no children attributed to her. Even though Lederman-Daniely freely admits the two characters "are not depicted as perceiving their self-realization in pregnancy and childbirth,"[5] she claims that they fulfill the role of "Great Mothers of the nation,"[6] describing their "motherhood" as part of "a female mode of being anchored in the female corporeality."[7] While Deborah does not fit the patriarchal notion of mother, she displays the "powerful leadership of unique qualities" of "women's culture" and illuminates "unforeseen facets of motherhood as a fierce force of

Judges, 112; and Webb, _The Book of the Judges_, 134.

3. Pierce, "Deborah," 3.

4. Skidmore-Hess and Skidmore-Hess, "Dousing the Fiery Woman," 6.

5. Lederman-Daniely, "'I Arose a Mother in Israel,'" 10. (Note that she implies that women can only reach "self-realization" through motherhood.)

6. Lederman-Daniely, "'I Arose a Mother in Israel,'" 10.

7. Lederman-Daniely, "'I Arose a Mother in Israel,'" 10.

leadership that brings the tide of change and transformation."[8] Even though Lederman-Daniely seems to be attempting a very feminist interpretation of Deborah, she actually continues to limit womanhood to the metaphor of motherhood and reproductive capacity.

Even J. Cheryl Exum, by including Deborah within her consideration of motherhood in the Hebrew Bible, participates in the "motherizing" of an otherwise childfree woman. She states, "Though we cannot be sure the text calls her a wife, it does call her a mother."[9] She goes on to describe Deborah's accomplishments, as found in Judg 4 and 5, as "counsel, inspiration, and protection" that clearly align with her definition of a "mother in Israel" as "one who brings liberation from oppression, provides protection, and ensures the well-being and security of her people."[10] While Exum's description of Deborah is somewhat accurate, she clearly limits these adjectives to what fits within her paradigm of motherhood. We can also describe Deborah as bold, brave, strong, and even militaristic, based on the texts, but these descriptors would not present Deborah within the traditional stereotypes of motherhood, or womanhood, for that matter. While Exum writes that Deborah's inclusion was an attempt to call "attention by contrast to the more usual position of women bound by patriarchal strictures,"[11] by insisting that Deborah is a mother, she has limited her character to those very same patriarchal strictures.

In Judg 4, Deborah is never described as a mother but is given two titles usually reserved for men: judge and prophet. By commanding Barak to launch a military offensive against Sisera's forces, and then accompanying him and the troops into battle, Deborah also is shown in a role that is even rarer for women in the Hebrew Bible: warrior.[12] Her character, as presented in Judg 4 and 5, is very complex but as Tikva Frymer-Kensky points out, "the rest of her legend is unrecorded and unpreserved."[13] In approaching Deborah's story, we must remember that it is contained within a text with a clear androcentric focus that tells the stories of the male judges who saved the Israelites from oppression at the hand of an enemy. While there is clearly more behind what we read about Deborah, we should be

---

8. Lederman-Daniely, "'I Arose a Mother in Israel,'" 10.

9. Exum, "'Mother in Israel,'" 85.

10. Exum, "'Mother in Israel,'" 85.

11. Exum, "'Mother in Israel,'" 85.

12. Other ANE cultures do portray women as warriors.

13. Frymer-Kensky, *Studies in Bible and Feminist Criticism*, 47.

(handwritten margin notes: Important Role Not based on Reproduction Only Major focus or view → reproduction)

aware of the fact that "neither the story nor the Song was framed as a record of Deborah's life . . .: it is a memory of Israel's defeat of Canaan, a defeat in which Deborah played an important role. Only this role is remembered, and when the action begins, Deborah is already in mid-career."[14] One thing is perfectly clear: Deborah's importance to the story within the Hebrew Bible is not based on her reproductive capabilities.

Deborah as Judge and Prophet—Judges 4:1–5

> 1 The Israelites again did what was evil in the sight of the Lord, after Ehud died. 2 So the Lord sold them into the hand of King Jabin of Canaan, who reigned in Hazor; the commander of his army was Sisera, who lived in Harosheth-ha-goiim. 3 Then the Israelites cried out to the Lord for help; for he had nine hundred chariots of iron, and had oppressed the Israelites cruelly twenty years. 4 At that time Deborah, a prophetess, wife of Lappidoth, was judging Israel. 5 She used to sit under the palm of Deborah between Ramah and Bethel in the hill country of Ephraim; and the Israelites came up to her for judgment.

The book of Judges follows a very obvious repetitive pattern of apostasy-oppression-repentance-salvation. The Israelites are described as doing "what was offensive to the Lord" and being oppressed by a foreign power. When the people finally cry out and repent, the Lord sends a judge to rescue them from the hand of the enemy. As stated above, the story of Deborah follows the pattern with one exception: there is no description of the Lord "raising up" a hero. Clearly, though, the storyteller intends for chapter 4 to be seen as a parallel to the preceding stories of Israel's judges, obvious in the opening three verses. Deborah's introduction is slightly different, but this is because Deborah is a rather unique leader of the Israelites. She fulfills the roles of judge and prophet, according to the first four verses of Judges 4.

In the majority of Bible translations, Deborah is also identified as the wife of Lappidoth. Other scholars[15] have already provided solid exegesis of the phrase 'eshet lapidoth, suggesting that a better translation might be fiery woman or woman of lightning, rather than a statement that Deborah is married to a man named, Lappidoth. Among the arguments

14. Frymer-Kensky, *Studies in Bible and Feminist Criticism*, 47.

15. See, for example, Ackerman, *Warrior, Dancer, Seductress, Queen.*

provided, the more convincing ones rely on the Hebrew usage of *'ishah* and the typical Hebrew form of proper names for men.

In biblical Hebrew there is no distinctive word for "wife"; rather, the word *'ishah*,[16] typically understood to have the broad meaning of "woman," is used in phrases where context indicates that the "woman" is actually the "wife" of some man (*'ish*). The fact that there is no Hebrew word used in the biblical texts that means exclusively "wife" is directly related to the lack of a Hebrew word for "marry." Most often the verb *la'qach* is used to indicate that a man "takes" a woman as a partner, much the same as one would "take" property or other inanimate objects. In many aspects, women were considered the property of males in ancient Israel. A female was the property of her father (and brothers) until she became the property of her husband. The verb *na'tan* is also utilized to indicate that her father "gives" her to another man, again in the sense of one giving an inanimate object.[17]

In the case of Deborah, the construct form of the word "woman" is used to indicate that there is a relationship with the word that follows, *lappidoth*. Scholars have pointed out that the word is not used anywhere else in the Hebrew Bible as a proper name. Also, the fact that it is used here in the feminine plural form would argue against it indicating the name of a male. In addition, the expected reference to "Lappidoth's" father is missing from the phrase.[18] This word is more commonly used to indicate "flames" or "fire." As a common noun, *lappid/lappidim* is used elsewhere in the Hebrew Bible to indicate a "torch" (see Gen 15:17; Isa 62:1; Ezek 1:13; Nah 2:4; Zech 12:6; Job 41:19; Dan 10:6).

Given that there is no requirement that *'eshet* be rendered as "wife of," and that it does not seem appropriate to treat *lappidoth* as a proper noun, a more plausible translation would be that Deborah is a "woman of flames" or even a "fiery woman."[19] The story certainly portrays her as a woman with great passion for the Holy and for her people. She certainly seems to "light a fire" under Barak and the Israelites to motivate them into action. This

---

16. There is also no separate word for "husband"; typically, *'ish* is translated "husband" based on contextual clues. There is the usage of *ba'al* to mean both "lord" and "husband."

17. This provides explanation of the stringent laws against a woman committing adultery; another man is metaphorically "trespassing" against her father/brothers or "husband."

18. Pierce, "Deborah," 3.

19. There is evidence of her being presented as a "fiery woman" in rabbinical literature [see Talmud Bavli Megillah 14a].

description of Deborah could also suggest a "woman of torches," indicating that she lights the way for her people, showing how they can follow the path of righteousness. Deborah's fieriness inspires people and reminds them of their covenant with the Creator of Light.

Deborah is unique among the judges, beyond being the only female, in that she is portrayed filling the typical roles of a judge. We are given a description of how she provides "judgement" for those who came to her, as she held court under the "Palm of Deborah." (Judg 4:5). The storyteller even gives the address for her business office—"on the road between Ramah and Bethel in the hill country of Ephraim" (Judg 4:5) In many ways, this picture of Deborah as leader of her people is similar to how Moses is portrayed as a judge for the people in Exod 18. In the same way that people sought him out for counsel, they now come to Deborah for her wisdom. While it is quite common for scholars to make a connection between Miriam and Deborah, Bruce Herzberg makes a strong case that a better parallel for Deborah would be Moses.[20] Utilizing the information provided about Deborah in Judg 4 and 5, he concludes that the biblical storytellers and writers intended to present her as being among the prophets like Moses whom the Holy promised to "raise up" (Exod 18:15–17).[21] In other words, Deborah was a "Moses of her time."[22]

Deborah as Prophet and Military Commander—Judges 4:6–9 and 14

6 She sent and summoned Barak son of Abinoam from Kedesh in Naphtali, and said to him, "The Lord, the God of Israel, commands you, 'Go, take position at Mount Tabor, bringing ten thousand from the tribe of Naphtali and the tribe of Zebulun. 7 I will draw out Sisera, the general of Jabin's army, to meet you by the Wadi Kishon with his chariots and his troops; and I will give him into your hand.'" 8 Barak said to her, "If you will go with me, I will go; but if you will not go with me, I will not go." 9 And she said, "I will surely go with you; nevertheless, the road on which you are going will not lead to your glory, for the Lord will sell Sisera into the hand of a woman." Then Deborah got up and went with Barak to Kedesh . . . 14 Then Deborah said to Barak, "Up! For this is the day on which the Lord has given Sisera into your hand. The Lord

20. Herzberg, "Deborah and Moses," 16.
21. Herzberg, "Deborah and Moses," 17.
22. Herzberg, "Deborah and Moses," 31.

is indeed going out before you." So Barak went down from Mount Tabor with ten thousand warriors following him.

Deborah is the second named woman given the title of prophet, and she does fulfill this role in a more traditional way than Miriam does. She is portrayed as delivering a divine message to Barak about going to battle against Sisera, the commander of King Jabin's army, assuring Barak of a victory (Judg 4:6–7). As with all of the female prophets in the Hebrew Bible, we do not get a call story for Deborah, but it is clear that she receives a word from the Holy. Like every good prophet, she delivers the prophecy with boldness and courage. What she has to tell Barak is an unbelievable idea. King Jabin's army is better equipped, having the advantage of chariots, and more powerful than any ragtag group of ten thousand men that Barak could put together at the last minute. In true prophetic form, Deborah is doubted by the recipient of the Divine command (Judg 4:8). It is quite common for prophets to be asked for some proof that they are a true messenger of the Holy. While Moses is given "magic tricks" to prove his merit (Exod 4:1–8), Deborah is required to do much more. Barak agrees to follow the orders of the Lord, but only if Deborah puts her life where her mouth is. He tests her commitment behind this prophecy, and she agrees to go into battle. However, she also warns Barak that he will not get the credit for the defeat of the enemy. She predicts that a woman will be the hero of the battle (Judg 4:9). While the obvious explanation seems to be that Deborah will be the victor, we learn later in the story that this female warrior is Jael (Judg 4:17–22). Even so, Deborah is also portrayed as a military leader in that she is able to command Barak, and she goes into battle with him and the troops as assurance. While this is the first time in the Hebrew Bible that a woman is placed in a military role as a warrior, it is not an unheard-of role for women in the ancient Near East.

Deborah as Poet-Singer—Judges 5:1–6

1 Then Deborah and Barak son of Abinoam sang on that day, saying:
2 "When locks are long in Israel,
   when the people offer themselves willingly—
   bless the Lord!

Judg 5:1-18
Moses Exodus 15:1-21
Miriam Exodus 15:20-21

3 "Hear, O kings; give ear, O princes;
 to the LORD I will sing,
  I will make melody to the LORD, the God of Israel.

4 "LORD, when you went out from Seir,
 when you marched from the region of Edom,
  the earth trembled, and the heavens poured,
   the clouds indeed poured water.
5 The mountains quaked before the LORD, the One of Sinai,
 before the LORD, the God of Israel.

6 "In the days of Shamgar son of Anath,
 in the days of Jael, caravans ceased
  and travelers kept to the byways."

In Judges 5, we find a song attributed to Deborah and Barak, recounting in poetic form the Israelites' liberation from the control of King Jabin. In this passage, Deborah is not described as a judge, nor is she specifically given the title of prophet, though her singing a song does align with Miriam's prophetic act in Exod 15:20–21. Her role as a military commander and warrior is present in the poetic text, where she is described as leading Issachar into battle (Judg 5:15).

Most scholars identify this hymn as a victory song, a genre usually associated with women (like Miriam) who greet warriors with a celebration of their military defeat of the enemy. However, some have questioned this labeling of Judg 5, noting that typically victory songs are sung to give praise to the Divine and declare that the victory was not really a human one but a Holy one. In Deborah and Barak's song, the victory is attributed primarily to human actors (Deborah, Jael, and Barak) and only secondarily to the Divine. The other unique aspect of this hymn is that it is sung by a military leader and not by the women who have been left behind, waiting for the men—husbands, fathers, sons, and brothers—to return from battle.

Deborah's song (Judg 5) parallels the song attributed to Moses (Exod 15:1–18) more than it does the song attributed to Miriam (Exod 15:20–21). It could be that the biblical editors intended to make Judg 5 an opportunity to remember the victory at the *Yam'suf.* In both stories the enemy clearly has the upper hand, but with divine intervention, water is the factor that secures the Israelites' liberation from a foreign power. Whereas in the story of the exodus, the Sea of Reeds clears a path for the escaped slaves to cross and then swallows Pharaoh's warriors (Exod 14), in the story of Deborah,

Barak, Sisera, and King Jabin's army (Judg 4), the dry riverbed suddenly becomes a torrent and sweeps away Sisera's men. The Israelites are victorious, and Deborah is celebrated as a hero, along with Jael and Barak. It would seem that Deborah is a sister to Miriam and the other women who carry out the ritual celebration of battle successes, but she is also unique in that she is on the battlefield and leads troops into battle.

Deborah as "Mother in Israel"—Judges 5:7

7 Deliverance ceased, Ceased in Israel, Till you arose, O Deborah, Arose, O mother, in Israel!

[handwritten margin note: Deborah delivered Israel]

A new title is given to Deborah in Judg 5:7, which states that she arose as a "mother in Israel" (or "O, Mother of Israel"). Should we interpret this to mean that indeed Deborah did have children, that she was a biological mother? Or is this a symbolic use of the term "mother"? This phrase, *'em b'israel*, occurs only one other place in the Hebrew Bible (2 Sam 20:19), where it is used to describe a city and not a woman. Here we find the story of Joab, King David's military commander, in his pursuit of Sheba, who leads a revolt against David. He corners Sheba in a small town, Abel, and is besieging that town, when the wise woman of the community confronts Joab about his attempted destruction of Abel, which she describes as "a mother in Israel."

Several scholars have spilled ink over the understanding of this title, "mother in Israel." Claudia Camp has argued that not only is the city of Abel a "mother in Israel," but the title should be given to the wise woman in Abel. Camp's conclusion is that what makes the wise woman a "mother in Israel" is her being a good counselor, her using powers of persuasion and negotiation to protect the Lord's heritage, her stepping forward willingly as a commander to lead the people in military battles, and her always seeking the unity and covenantal shalom of God's people. Susan Ackerman builds on Camp's conclusions about the wise woman of Abel to argue that this description of a "mother in Israel" applies to Deborah as well: she is known for her counseling skills (as a judge), she leads her people in battle, and she is concerned for the well-being of Israel.[23]

This understanding of "mother of/in Israel" makes it is clear that the title does not imply a biological experience. We can then determine that

23. Camp, "The Wise Women of 2 Samuel." See also Ackerman, *Warrior, Dancer, Seductress, Queen*, 42–43.

Is to prove childless?

Deborah is not being described as a woman with children. Still, the question remains; why is this label used? Is it possible that the poem wants to legitimate Deborah's importance by attributing to her a more traditional role in Israelite society? If Deborah is not a wife or a mother in the traditional sense, can this also be related to her ability to fulfill the roles of judge, prophet, and warrior? Does her status as childfree allow Deborah to be available for the people who seek her wisdom? Does this help her to be open to the voice of the Divine and available to deliver the prophecy to wherever the Holy sends her? Does this give her the freedom to go into battle, without concern for leaving her children orphaned?

Deborah as Military Commander and Warrior—Judges 5:12–15

> 12 "Awake, awake, Deborah! Awake, awake, utter a song! Arise, Barak, lead away your captives, O son of Abinoam. 13 Then down marched the remnant of the noble; the people of the Lord marched down for him against the mighty. 14 From Ephraim they set out into the valley, following you, Benjamin, with your kin; from Machir marched down the commanders, and from Zebulun those who bear the marshal's staff; 15 the chiefs of Issachar came with Deborah, and Issachar faithful to Barak; into the valley they rushed out at his heels. Among the clans of Reuben there were great searchings of heart.

As indicated above, some have questioned whether Deborah actually led troops into battle or simply was a cheerleader on the sidelines, encouraging and inspiring the team. The poetic telling of the victory over Sisera leaves no doubt about her role as military commander and warrior. In the midst of describing the different tribes' responses to participation in the battle, v. 15 states that "Issachar's chiefs were with Deborah." This phrase is synonymously paralleled by the second phrase, "As Barak, so was Issachar": together the phrases indicate that both Issachar and Barak were in battle with Deborah.

This image of a female warrior is unique in the Hebrew Bible, or at least it seems to be. Whenever Israelite forces go into battle, a masculine plural noun or pronoun is used in translation, rendered as "men," "they," or "them." This use of the word *anashim* could be intended to include only men, but there are times that the same word indicates a mixed group of men and women. The same is true for the use of masculine plural pronouns.[24] Thus, just because the masculine plural forms of the noun or pronoun are used to describe the soldiers or warriors of Israel, it does not exclude the possibility of some women being included in the group. In fact there is some evidence that peoples surrounding ancient Israel had females who fought in battle so perhaps Israel was not a stranger to this practice.[25]

In her article "By the Hand of a Woman," Gale Yee discusses how the sociological context of premonarchic Israel could have dictated that women fight in the battles against enemies. "Certain aspects of pre-monarchic Israelite society would have made female leadership in war possible. In contrast to the time of the monarchy, no centralized bureaucracy, focusing on a king, governed the independent tribes. Instead, social relationships were based on strong kinship and residential ties."[26] Yee goes on to argue that women during this time of Israel's story "had opportunities to take up leadership in war precisely because military organization was essentially domestic in character."[27] She even mentions specifically Deborah as an example of a female military leader. The chaos described in the book of Judges might well have allowed for women (and others) to step into roles, according to their gifts, that had not earlier been and would not later be available to them. So for instance when a stable government might come into place again, those who normally hold these positions expect to resume them and have the temporary substitutes return to lower-profile roles.[28]

Another factor might give credence to Deborah's being understood as a warrior in Israel's story. Some scholars have pointed out what they see as similarities between Deborah and the Canaanite goddess Anat. While Israel was strictly prohibited from conceiving of their god in a human form, their neighbors most often worshiped a pantheon of deities.[29] Each deity

24. For example, Gen 17:23. David Stein has a very solid analysis of the meaning of 'anashim in Stein, "What Does It Mean to Be a 'Man'?"

25. See pages 26-27, above, along with footnotes 44-51.

26. Yee, "By the Hand of a Woman," 110.

27. Yee, "By the Hand of a Woman," 111.

28. In the United States, this idea is best portrayed in the image of Rosie the Riveter, who represented the women who stepped into what were traditionally male jobs during World War II. Likewise, these women were expected to abandon these jobs in order for the returning soldiers to have a position in society.

29. It is quite common in the scholarship of the Hebrew Bible to admit that Israel's monotheism was a late development and that Israelites were polytheists at first. When Israel made the commitment to one deity, the characteristics of all the gods (whether

was responsible for a certain aspect of life (e.g., storms and rain, fertility, war, and so forth). Most often readers of the Hebrew Bible are familiar with the so-called fertility goddesses that were seen as a constant threat to Israel's worship of only one God. In fact, a common misunderstanding is that all female deities were fertility goddesses, and also mothers. However, there were goddesses in the ancient Near East whose surrounding mythology did not portray them as mothers or even as primarily overseeing domestic concerns. For example, there were goddesses of war known for their courage and battle skills. Among them was Anat.

The parallels between Deborah and Anat have been identified in other places,[30] so we will just look at those that are easiest to see. First, both Deborah and Anat have a subordinate male who carries out her demands. Deborah's was Barak, and Anat's was Yatpan. Both female characters are celebrated for their bravery and portrayed as going into battle for their people. P.C. Craigie has argued that "the poetic imagery of Anat [was] associated with Deborah,"[31] especially the imagery of Anat as warrior in the heavens and of Deborah as warrior on earth. Both females inspire troops through their charisma and are portrayed as independent, without a husband or children.[32]

Does the fact that the ancient Israelites may have been familiar with a warrior goddess mean that they actually could image women as warriors? There is clearly a link between metaphors used for the Holy and human roles within society. Does the resemblance between Deborah and Anat suggest that the biblical writers also had knowledge of women who went to battle? Would that have been possible? Surprisingly, the archeology of Israel during the Iron I period seems to support this possibility. Carol Meyers, in her work on women in Israel and as an archeologist, has concluded that the ethnographic and sociological studies of the findings dating to this period remarkably coincide with the sociohistorical background found in Judges. While most scholars date the final version of this biblical book to a much later period, some of these legends could have originated in this earlier phase of Israel's development. And there is some consensus that the

male or female) were included in the metaphorical language used to describe the Holy One of Israel (e.g., warrior, midwife, Lord, rock, and so forth). This is why there are so many different, and often conflicting, divine images found in the Hebrew Bible.

30. See Craigie, "Deborah and Anat"; and Taylor, "The Song of Deborah and Two Canaanite Goddesses."

31. Craigie, "Deborah and Anat," 375.

32. Craigie, "Deborah and Anat," 377–78.

song in Judg 5 can be dated to 1100 BCE, which places it in or close to the Iron 1 age. Meyers' work has made the case that "in the domestically-based premonarchic era of Ancient Israelite history, women would have been integrally involved in their community's economic, social, political, and religious affairs."[33] There seems to be no reason not to extend this to include the community's defenses.

While there is no clear evidence that Deborah existed historically, she did exist in the imaginations of the communities behind the biblical texts. This could suggest that she represents ancient women who actually fulfilled the role of warrior, as well as judge and prophet. If, as is generally assumed, most responsibility for raising children was given to women, and if mothers generally nursed their own babies and perhaps found themselves pregnant on a regular basis during their fertile years, these women did not likely go into battle. However, women who were childfree, like Deborah, would be ready and able to leave home and engage in war. Not only would such women not be limited by pregnancy and nursing, but they would also leave no dependents behind to be potentially orphaned. When the call to war came, both men and women responded. It is even possible to imagine that the battle cry might have come from a female warrior.

Deborah—A Childfree Woman

As has been presented above, there is no reason to read Deborah as a wife or mother. The support for translating *lappidot* as her husband's name has no grounding in grammar or contextual clues. Even though "mother" is used in reference to Deborah in Judg 5, scholars have made a strong case for understanding this as an honorific title (perhaps even connected to the military) and not a biological declaration. What is clear in the texts of Judg 4 and 5 is that the character of Deborah is portrayed as a judge, prophet, poet-singer, and warrior. No semantic or grammatical gymnastics are necessary to reach this conclusion. In the story of Judges, Deborah is a passionate leader of Israel during a tumultuous time, who demonstrates her divinely inspired wisdom and courage on behalf of her people. Her place as a childfree woman among Israel's stories cannot be erased, despite interpreters' attempts to domesticate her. Her flame burns too bright.

---

33 Ackerman, "Digging Up Deborah," 175.

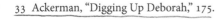

A Word about Jael (Judg 4:17–24, 5:24–27)—Host, Assassin, Hero

Although her story is surrounded by that of Deborah, Jael is another powerful woman who takes matters in her own hands and defeats the Israelite enemy, Sisera (Judg 4:17–22). The Divine providence holds true in the Israelite's military success over King Jabin's army. Through both human and natural acts, the unlikely ragtag army is able to beat a much more powerful foe with the best military technology. As the Canaanite soldiers are losing their lives on the battlefield, their defeat is imminent, and the commander, Sisera, runs for safety. Seeking shelter from the Israelite soldiers who are hot on his tail, he comes to the tent of Heber the Kenite; however, the "man of the house" is not home. Instead, he encounters Jael and probably sees this as a great opportunity. No woman on her own could deny Sisera's demands. He mistakenly sees Jael as weak and helpless. She gives him more than he expects.

Like the names of many Hebrew Bible characters, Jael's name has possible meanings that reflect her role in the story. Most understand *ya'el* to mean "wild goat"; thus, she is an untamed woman who acts in what may be considered unconventional ways. Another way of translating her name is to read it as *ya'el* and translate it as "YHWH is God." This might indicate the great faith that Jael had and her action reflecting the strength of the Holy. One more possible rendering of her name is "he/it helped," which seems a bit odd because Jael is portrayed as female.[34] Whatever her name is taken to mean, it is certain that Jael plays a key role in the Israelites' defeat of Sisera and King Jabin's army. She takes drastic and decisive action to help them achieve a period of rest from foreign oppression.

Jael is introduced as the "wife" or "woman" of Heber the Kenite (Judg 4:17). With the insider information about the relationship between King Jabin and Heber's clan, we and Sisera assume that this is a safe place. But, why is Jael home alone? Given the treaty between Heber and Sisera, it is possible that Heber is fighting (and dying?) with Sisera's army, leaving Jael all alone. Halpern has suggested that Heber is a double agent, aligning with both Israel and King Jabin.[35] There is another possibility that revolves around how one interprets the phrase *'eshet heber*. As we said about the way Deborah is introduced, does this phrase mean that Jael is the "wife

---

34. Some scholars have pointed to this masculine verb form perhaps being an indication of Jael's "gender-bending" (i.e., acting in ways usually associated with a male). See, e.g., Duran, *Having Men for Dinner*, 18.

35. Halpern, *The First Historians*, 85-87.

of" Heber, or could it mean that she is "a woman of the Heber clan"?[36] This possible second meaning of *'eshet heber* could explain why the tent is described as belonging to Jael and not Heber.

While Jael's marital status is unclear, there is absolutely no indication that she is a mother. Although no children are mentioned, scholars have spent many words describing how Jael acts like a mother (as well as a seductress).[37] Instead of seeing her behavior as following the hospitality codes prevalent at the time, they frame her behavior within an assumption of motherhood, based on essentialist ideas of womanhood. When these same actions are taken by Abraham, he is celebrated as the epitome of hospitality (Gen 18:1–8), so why is this behavior by a female character evaluated differently? Granted, Jael does not fulfill the promise of protection inherent within an offer of hospitality; however, the final outcome is carried out in a way that aligns with actions of an assassin rather than of a mother or a seductress. Some have argued that Jael's giving Sisera milk rather than the water he requests clearly indicates that we should see Jael as performing motherhood.[38] Another scholar argues that the final scene, when Jael shows Barak the slain Sisera, "is suggestive of the man finally being welcomed into the women's quarters to see the child that has been born."[39] Even if Jael's childfree status were named (it is not, and naming this status would be unique in the Hebrew Bible), commentators still would want to (and do) assign to her the attitudes and acts of a mother. One wonders, though, why interpreters cannot just accept that Jael is a hospitable host, assassin, and military hero; that is enough.

I am Deborah . . .

I settled your disputes, . . . but that was not enough.

I delivered the Holy's words, . . . but that was not enough.

I led you to a military defeat of the enemy, . . . but that was not enough.

So, you labeled me a mother, . . . and I was enough for you.

I was a fiery woman, . . . and I am a part of the story.

36. Schneider, *Judges*, 77.

37. See Sasson, "'A Breeder or Two for Each Leader'"; Yee, "By the Hand of a Woman"; and Exum, "Feminist Criticism."

38. Sasson, "'A Breeder or Two for Each Leader,'" 343.

39. Tamber-Rosenau, "Striking Women," 135.

5

HULDAH

Prophet, Scribe, Priest, Interpreter, Canonizer,
and Reformer

Introducing Huldah

At one of the most crucial moments of Judah's history, the ruler of the nation relies on the advice of a previously unknown woman. In a male-dominated society, such an unprecedented move demands our consideration. Given the many male voices to which King Josiah could have listened, why would he choose Huldah? While many today do not know much, if anything, about Huldah, she obviously was better known in her day. Perhaps Huldah is a key figure in understanding the subversive presence of female religious leaders within the male-dominated religious cult in Jerusalem. She represents the countless wise women who when the time was right have quietly provided a needed word among those who clamor for attention.

The story about Huldah and her role in King Josiah's reforms is found in 2 Kgs 22:14–20 with a parallel account in 2 Chr 34:22–28; both accounts agree on the basic information about her, at least on what little bit the Hebrew Bible provides. In each she is identified as a prophet, the third named female prophet (the fourth is Noadiah, mentioned in Neh 6:14). Given Huldah's role in these texts, we might also conclude that she was literate and could have been a scribe. Huldah is also introduced as the wife of Shallum, who is the royal wardrobe keeper. She's the prophet; Shallum is the wardrobe keeper in the palace. She is consulted on matters of theology and authority; Shallum does the laundry.

While the choice of a female for such an important task may seem surprising, again the text does not explain that Huldah is chosen because a male prophet is not available or, as rabbinic commentators have suggested, because the king's men thought a woman would give a gentler answer. If the latter is the true motivation, then Hilkiah and the others do not get what they want. Huldah's message for the people of Judah is as harsh as the words of Amos or Jeremiah. In order to fulfill her task as a prophet, Huldah must have been educated, known to the high priest, and readily available to advise the king on important matters. None of what the character of Huldah encompasses includes the role of mother.

Huldah as Interpreter of Texts and as Scribe—2 Kings 22:8–14

8 The high priest Hilkiah said to Shaphan the secretary, "I have found the book of the law in the house of the Lord." When Hilkiah gave the book to Shaphan, he read it. 9 Then Shaphan the secretary came to the king, and reported to the king, "Your servants have emptied out the money that was found in the house, and have delivered it into the hand of the workers who have oversight of the house of the Lord." 10 Shaphan the secretary informed the king, "The priest Hilkiah has given me a book." Shaphan then read it aloud to the king. 11 When the king heard the words of the book of the law, he tore his clothes. 12 Then the king commanded the priest Hilkiah, Ahikam son of Shaphan, Achbor son of Micaiah, Shaphan the secretary, and the king's servant Asaiah, saying, 13 "Go, inquire of the Lord for me, for the people, and for all Judah, concerning the words of this book that has been found; for great is the wrath of the Lord that is kindled against us, because our ancestors did not obey the words of this book, to do according to all that is written concerning us." 14 So the priest Hilkiah, and Ahikam, Achbor, Shaphan, and Asaiah went to the prophetess Huldah—the wife of Shallum son of Tikvah son of Harhas, the keeper of the wardrobe—who was living in Jerusalem in the Mishneh, and they spoke to her.

Second Kings is part of what scholars commonly refer to as the Deuteronomistic History, which includes the material from Joshua to 2 Kings.

A German scholar of the Hebrew Bible, Martin Noth, put forth the theory that these biblical books were the work of one writer-composer, who sought to record a history of Israel during the Babylonian exile. Since Noth's time, scholars have come to envision the creation of this history as the work of more than one person, perhaps of a school or at least of a group of like-minded people. Utilizing a variety of sources, the Deuteronomistic historians retell Israel's story, from emergence in the promise land until the fall of Jerusalem, pointing out where the people went wrong and made mistakes that eventually led to the exile (e.g., choosing a human ruler over God, worshiping other gods, failing to care for the vulnerable, and so forth). Since this recounting was done through hindsight, which is usually twenty-twenty, the compilers are able to clearly identify what they determine to be bad decisions and ways that the people broke covenant with God and with one another. We must remember, though, that this version of Israel's history is told from the perspective of the powerful, and thus it represents only one view of how the events leading to the exile unfolded.

In 2 Kgs 22, we read about the reign of King Josiah, the last righteous ruler of Judah (see 2 Kgs 23:25). Although he takes the throne at a young age, Josiah is portrayed as a wise and faithful ruler who seeks to correct the terrible apostasy that has been tolerated and even encouraged by a preceding king, Manasseh. Josiah's reforms are centered on reforming the temple in Jerusalem, ridding it of idols and restoring it as the place of worship for Israel's one God. Amid the royally ordered spring cleaning, a book is discovered that is the key to what happens in the remainder of the chapter (2 Kgs 22:3–8). The Bible does not tell us what it is about this scroll, the first recorded archaeological find, that makes the workers save it from the trash heap, but they do. The scroll is given to Hilkiah the priest, who also recognizes its importance and passes it along to the king's secretary, Shaphan, who brings it to the palace, and upon Josiah's request, Shaphan reads the scroll aloud (2 Kgs 22:9–10).

Whatever that the scroll contained causes Josiah to tear his clothes (2 Kgs 22:11). In the biblical world, this was the expected response when one received some really bad news. Josiah realizes that the people of Judah have not abided by the words of the scroll and that if the book is authentic, the whole place is doomed. Josiah orders a group of five men, including Shaphan and Hilkiah, to go and inquire of the Lord about what the scroll says. He wants them to verify its legitimacy, or more likely, he hopes to discover that the scroll is a fake so that he can disregard its condemnation.

The group seeks out a previously unknown woman to make this life-or-death pronouncement. They take the king's inquiry straight to Huldah (2 Kgs 22:14).

The introduction of Huldah into the story provides a basic pedigree for her. We are given her title, "the prophet," the name of her husband, Shallum, a bit of his family tree, and where she lives. We do not learn anything about her family of origin, which is not surprising given the Bible's focus primarily on male genealogy. Huldah is married, and her husband has a position within the royal court. The nature of that role is unclear. Some have suggested that Shallum is connected to the cult, and others understand him to be more a servant of the king. His occupation is not important to the story; Huldah is the one whom the men are seeking. The fact that Huldah and her husband live in the Second Quarter (Mishneh) of Jerusalem has caused scholarly speculation. Typically, this section of the city is understood as a new addition to Jerusalem, perhaps even for an enclave of wealthier citizens. Such a suggestion is based on the basic meaning of the Hebrew word *Mishneh* as "addition."[1] However, Judith McKinlay argues that Huldah's location in the Mishneh was intended to indicate that she is outside the temple area. Even though she is a prophet, her being female means that she cannot defile the sacred space. Her location demarks "the clearly secondary status of the woman Huldah to that of the men who could enter the temple."[2]

Another way of interpreting Huldah's location, and perhaps a more fitting one, is to link the word *mishneh* with the word *Mishnah*, which means "to study" in Hebrew. In the King James Version, this word *mishneh* is translated as "college" in 2 Kgs 22:14 ("she dwelt in Jerusalem in the college") and has led to interpretive speculation that Huldah was a professor, specifically a "professor of jurisprudence or of the languages,"[3] according to Elizabeth Cady Stanton. In her presentation of Huldah, Stanton elevates her to a status as "the greatest of women in the history of Judah or Israel," with an unrivaled legal mind.[4] Others have described Huldah as a librarian, legislator, and "teacher of the male establishment."[5]

---

1. Ilan, "Huldah," 9.
2. Handy, "Reading Huldah," 26.
3. Stanton, *The Original Feminist Attack*, 81.
4. Stanton, *The Original Feminist Attack*, 82.
5. Trible, "Huldah's Holy Writ," 10.

At the bare minimum, we can see Huldah as a prophet and a scholar who lives in a place of learning. In fact, this understanding of her address is fairly common in early rabbinic commentary and in Jewish legend, which envisions Huldah as a teacher to whom people came for wisdom and learning. The Targum of Jonathon states that Huldah "sat in a house of study."[6] The rabbis taught that she ran a school in Jerusalem, and there has been the suggestion that Josiah was a student of hers. From early in the history of Jerusalem, there were two gates within the city wall that were associated with Huldah, and the traditional location of her burial was a sacred site.[7] She clearly left an impression that lasted beyond the biblical story.

While Huldah is introduced first as "the prophet" (2 Kgs 22:14), it is important to stop and consider what is required of her to determine whether the scroll is divinely inspired. While the text does not specifically state that they give the scroll to Huldah, it makes sense that she needs to see the words for herself in order to declare it authentic or not. It follows, then, that Huldah is literate; she can read and is deemed capable of interpreting the words on the papyrus. While rabbinic tradition has long considered Huldah to have been a scribe, many have missed this role that she fulfills. In fact, it has been suggested that the reason the king's envoy seeks out Huldah, rather than a better-known prophet such as Jeremiah, is that she can read whereas Jeremiah required the skills of his scribe, Baruch.

Huldah as Prophet, Priest, Canonizer, and Reformer—2 Kings 22:15–20

> 15 She declared to them, "Thus says the LORD, the God of Israel: Tell the man who sent you to me, 16 Thus says the LORD, I will indeed bring disaster on this place and on its inhabitants—all the words of the book that the king of Judah has read. 17 Because they have abandoned me and have made offerings to other gods, so that they have provoked me to anger with all the work of their hands, therefore my wrath will be kindled against this place, and it will not be quenched. 18 But as to the king of Judah, who sent you to inquire of the Lord, thus shall you say to him, Thus says the LORD, the God of Israel: Regarding the words that you have heard, 19 because your heart was penitent, and you humbled yourself before the LORD, when you heard how I spoke against this place, and

6. Cohn, "Rabbi Huldah."
7. Cohn, "Rabbi Huldah."

against its inhabitants, that they should become a desolation and a curse, and because you have torn your clothes and wept before me, I also have heard you, says the LORD. 20 Therefore, I will gather you to your ancestors, and you shall be gathered to your grave in peace; your eyes shall not see all the disaster that I will bring on this place." They took the message back to the king.

Having been identified as a prophet in the introduction, Huldah now performs her role by responding to the question about the scroll's authenticity with a prophetic message. As compared with the other female prophets in the Hebrew Bible, Huldah and her words align most closely to what most of us associate with the word *prophet*. In fact, she delivers two different prophecies: one for the people of Judah and one for Josiah. She does not sugarcoat her words of judgment. Whatever the words on the scroll were, it seems most likely they included part of the covenant the Divine made with the Israelites as recorded in the Torah, but especially in Deuteronomy with its lists of blessings for keeping covenant and its curses for breaking it. According to the biblical story, the people had agreed to keep all of the commandments given to them by the Holy through Moses, understanding the consequences of failing to do so. At this point in 2 Kings, there have been centuries of the people worshiping other deities and failing to take care of the least of these. Each generation had heard prophets reminding them of their commitments and offering them the opportunity to change—to recommit themselves to the covenant their ancestors had made in the wilderness. Now, as the people face the overwhelming threat of a foreign enemy, their unfaithful behavior has led them to a place of no return. However, the Divine offers them one more chance through yet another prophetic voice and through the king's reforms.

Huldah frames her prophecies in the same way other prophets had, with "Thus says the Lord the God of Israel." This short messenger formula is common in the prophetic texts; it provides an identification of the deity for whom the prophet speaks and an authentication that the prophet is speaking with authority.[8] Her first message, for the people of Judah, is a prophetic announcement of judgment. Many of the preexilic prophets deliver such words of judgment, followed by an image of what the consequence will be for the people's breaking their covenant with the Holy and with one another. Huldah is actually the first biblical prophet "unequivocally to declare

---

8 Westermann, *Basic Forms of Prophetic Speech*, 102–3.

the immanent destruction of the state of Judah and unquestioningly to be believed."[9]

Many scholars have noted similarities between this prophecy of Huldah and those of Jeremiah, who is never mentioned in 2 Kings. Some, like Robert Wilson, have even suggested that Jeremiah and Huldah were related, perhaps nephew and aunt, respectively.[10] The words attributed to Huldah, "Thus says the LORD, I will indeed bring disaster on this place and on its inhabitants" (2 Kgs 22:16), are found in only one other place in the Hebrew Bible. The same combination is found in Jer 19:3, in his prophecy about the coming destruction of Jerusalem.[11] It is not surprising though that there would be similarities between Huldah and Jeremiah, given that they both appear against the backdrop of the seventh century BCE, after the fall of the Northern Kingdom, and facing the frightening reality that Judah will suffer the same fate, if not at the hand of Assyria, then by the next major ancient Near Eastern power, Babylonia.

Huldah's prophetic message for Josiah, by contrast, is an announcement of salvation. While this form is less common among preexilic prophets, it can be found in each of the biblical prophets of the time period (i.e., Amos, Hosea, Micah, Isaiah 1–39, and even Jeremiah). More specifically, Huldah's words are directed to an individual and not the people as a whole. She tells Josiah's men to tell him that the Holy has recognized his faithfulness in seeking reforms in the land and his appropriate response to the hearing of the coming destruction. Josiah's attempts to be faithful to the covenant will result in his being spared the violence awaiting Judah. Instead, he will not witness the fall of Jerusalem but will go to his grave in peace (2 Kgs 22:18–20). These words of promise, however, do not play out according to the description of Josiah's death found in 2 Kgs 23:29, where the King of Egypt kills him.

This so-called failed prophecy of Huldah has led some to declare her a false prophet, one whose words do not come true.[12] However, this assertion requires a very limited understanding of the criteria for a true prophet, provided in Deut 13:1–5, 18:21. These passages describe a false prophet as one who leads the people to worship other gods, or whose words do not prove true. This last criterion does not require that the events described

---

9. Handy, "Reading Huldah," 32.

10. Wilson, *Prophecy and Society*, 219–23, 298.

11. Ilan, "Huldah," 8.

12. Ilan, "Huldah," 3.

in a prophet's message actually occur as described. Rather, the criterion of whether a prophet's words prove true has to do with whether the prophet's words are aligned with the covenantal relationship between Israel and the Divine. There is no evidence that either criterion is accurate in regard to Huldah's prophecy. In fact, those who produced 2 Kings clearly do not question her legitimacy. "If the author (or editor, as some would suggest) had truly been interested in the fact that the king died counter to the prophecy, it would follow that Huldah was a false prophet and Josiah should not have listened to her, but this clearly has not been the intent."[13] According to Tal Ilan, Huldah is "the ultimate Deuteronomic prophet, who utters the ultimate Deuteronomic prophecy of doom."[14]

Given the opening description of Huldah, she does not seem to fit the pattern of other itinerant or temporary prophets like Micah or Amos. These prophets are portrayed as outsiders, as peripheral prophets, and sometimes as itinerant messengers for a certain time period. However, because the biblical writers provide an address for Huldah (describing her as living in Jerusalem and married to some sort of court employee), scholars have offered different answers to the question of what type of prophet she was. Some have argued that she was obviously a court prophet, not only consulted by the king but also a royal employee.[15] According to Phyllis Trible, Huldah had a "superior status" within the kingdom. "The high priest and other leaders visit her; she is not summoned to appear before them."[16] Others have suggested that Huldah was a cult prophet[17] and perhaps connected to the worship of Asherah. This would make her support of Josiah's reforms self-incriminating because of his orders to erase the worship of false gods from the land.[18] However, there is no indication in the text that Huldah is connected to the worship of Asherah. In her prophecies, she clearly identifies the source of her words as the "LORD God of Israel." One tradition has argued that Huldah, like Josiah, is one of the few people in Jerusalem who has not been lured into apostasy. She worships only the God of Israel

13. Handy, "The Role of Huldah," 51.

14. Ilan, "Huldah," 3.

15. See for example Wilson, *Prophecy and Society*.

16. Trible, "Huldah's Holy Writ," 9.

17. Priest, "Huldah's Oracle," 367–68; Camp, "Huldah," 96.

18. McKinlay, in "Gazing at Huldah" argues that Huldah is a puppet of the Deuteronomist to show even a female (perhaps an Asherah prophet) determined that Israel's god was the only true deity and should be worshiped exclusively.

and follows the teachings of Moses, which makes her the best authority to determine the truth of the scroll found in the temple.

Lowell K. Handy and a few others have drawn attention to some intriguing parallels between the story of Huldah and literature from other ancient Near Eastern cultures about a certain type of prophet or priest. In the seventh century BCE, Assyrian kings employed female prophets who "often delivered messages concerning the safety of the king and the granting of divine protection against his enemies."[19] Thus, Josiah's seeking a word from the prophet Huldah would be a natural process. However, Handy argues for a stronger parallel between Huldah and Mesopotamian omen priests, who are consulted by royal intermediaries to "double-check" the desires of the gods about a ruler's plans for cultic reforms.[20] Although she is not given the title priest in 2 Kings, Handy states that in confirming "the contents of the scroll allegedly found in the temple, Huldah clearly plays the narrative role held by the priests of the omen deities."[21]

While many would be quick to argue that the commandments of Israel's covenant with the Divine did not allow for female priests, this argument about Huldah's role in the story having strong similarities to what omen priests did in cultures that influenced Israel seems to call such a quick conclusion into question. In addition to being a prophet, especially if we go with the idea of her being connected to the cult, could Huldah have been a priest? Whereas the Babylonian omen priests used signs in nature (e.g., bird flight patterns, animal entrails) to determine the will of the gods, Huldah read a text to provide divine justification for Josiah's reforms. Given the Divine's judgment of the people's behavior as unacceptable, Josiah had a stronger case for the religious reforms he wanted to put into place.

There is yet another unique characteristic to Huldah's prophetic role. She is the only prophet in the Hebrew Bible who gleans her message of judgment based on the exegesis of a written document.[22] Prior to this story, "revelation was conceived of as spoken words, a personal interaction between the prophet and God."[23] Karel van der Toorn points out that the designation of a written text as authoritative opens the door for revelation to be available to "scribes and scholars; the art of interpretation supplanted

---

19. Cogan and Tadmor, *II Kings*, 284.
20. Handy, "The Role of Huldah," 45.
21. Handy, "The Role of Huldah," 45.
22. Camp, "Huldah: Bible."
23. Cohn, "Rabbi Huldah."

the gift of intuition."[24] In her authentication of the scroll, Huldah also begins the long process of what we now describe as the canonization of Scripture.[25] If the scroll was some form of Deuteronomy, Huldah authorizes what would become part of the central focus of Judaism, the Torah.

I would also argue that Huldah was a reformer; her authentication of the scroll and her prophetic messages motivated Josiah's reforms. While some have pointed out that her prophecies never mention a reform[26] and should not be seen as related to what happens in 2 Kgs 23, others have suggested that Huldah actually broadened Josiah's understanding of what needed to be addressed in the reforms. The king had been primarily focused on restoring the temple and proper worship of the Divine, which was very important in order to correct one aspect of the broken covenant. However, Huldah's authorization of the scroll reminds Josiah that Israel's covenant with the Holy has both vertical and horizontal aspects. As many preexilic prophets declare, proper worship without proper ethics will not satisfy the Divine.[27] In that same tradition, Huldah initiates the social reform that would benefit the powerless and the marginalized.[28]

Huldah as Prophet, Interpreter, Priest, and Canonizer
—2 Chronicles 34

The books of 1 and 2 Chronicles recount the stories of Israel from the first human to the period of the Babylonian exile (596/86 BCE). The authors of this history wrote after the destruction of the Jerusalem temple in an effort to give a reason for why the descendants of Sarah and Abraham no longer ruled the land promised in the covenant the Divine had made with them. It is believed that the writers of this history used the Deuteronomistic History (Josh–2 Kgs), especially Samuel and Kings, as well as other sources to construct a different version of the demise of Israel. Like the Deuteronomistic History, Chronicles is written in hindsight and blames the exile on the people's unfaithfulness and their breaking the covenant, expressing a theology of reward and punishment, or "you reap what you sow." Chronicles, though, has a different perspective; the focus is on David and

24. Van der Toorn, *Scribal Culture*, 206–7.

25. Camp, "Huldah: Bible."

26. Handy, "The Role of Huldah," 52.

27. See Amos 5:21–24; Mic 6:1–8; Isa 1:1–17; and so forth.

28. Achtelstetter, "Huldah at the Table," 181–82.

his descendants. The stories told in Chronicles attempt to rehabilitate the image of the Davidic lineage (e.g., Chronicles omits the Bathsheba incident [2 Sam 11]) and try to explain away some seeming theological dilemmas found in Samuel and Kings (e.g., why Manasseh, the worst king of Judah, reigns the longest).

One of the major events in this history is the split of David's kingdom after Solomon's death into Israel (the Northern Kingdom) and Judah (the Southern Kingdom). While Judah enjoys the stability of the Davidic dynasty, Israel has a more tumultuous government, with multiple rulers sitting on the throne, some for extremely short reigns. Finally, in the eighth century (circa 722 BCE), Israel is conquered by Assyria, and the Northern Kingdom ceases to exist, leaving Judah to stand against the threat of foreign nations. However, Chronicles recounts only Judah's history, declaring the unfaithfulness of the tribes who secede from the united kingdom.

Second Chronicles 34:19–28 is another account of Huldah's authentication of the scroll found in the temple and her prophetic announcements. There are only two differences between this version and the one in 2 Kings 22. One difference handles a perceived theological dilemma from 2 Kings, and another difference seems to limit Huldah's role in Josiah's reforms. The first difference that we will consider is the theological one. As mentioned above, there has been a tendency to see Huldah's second prophecy, the announcement of salvation for Josiah, as false, since Josiah did not die peacefully, as Huldah's words seemed to indicate he would. For those behind the books of Chronicles, this was an inconsistency in Kings that needs to be corrected. Thus, we find in 2 Chr 35:20–24 an explanation of why Josiah is killed in battle; he chooses to engage King Neco in a fight, even though Neco warns Josiah that the Holy is on his side. In other words, Josiah refuses to listen to the prophetic words of the Egyptian king and thus suffers a fatal wound. This fits with the overall theme of Chronicles—that the consequences of individuals' (particularly rulers') going against the Divine's will are swift and personal.

In 2 Chr 34, Huldah is still presented as a prophet and perhaps priest, as well as scribe, interpreter of texts, and canonizer of holy texts. However, one role has been removed from her resume in this version; Huldah is not involved in instigating the reforms of Josiah. The Chronicles text is very specific that Josiah had begun his reforms long before Huldah was consulted about the scroll and delivered her prophecies. While 2 Chr 34:3 states that in the eighth year of his reign, Josiah "began to seek the God of his ancestor David" and in the twelfth year began to rid Judah of all vestiges of idolatry, it does not indicate that he "sought" a prophet or priest to know what reforms needed to be done. Given that Jeremiah is specifically mentioned as singing laments for Josiah upon his death, one might imagine that the writers and compilers of Chronicles have replaced Huldah's role as prophet of the reform with Jeremiah.

The heavy-handed editing of the material in Samuel and Kings by the authors of Chronicles seems to make two corrections to the portrayal of Huldah. On the one hand, Chronicles clears Huldah of any accusations of being a false prophet; we know why Josiah dies (2 Chr 35:20–24) in a way different than she imagines he will (2 Chr 34:26–28). On the other hand, we find in Chronicles the reduction of Huldah's role in the reforms that take place under the king. Clearly the first change from 2 Kings is made for theological reasons, but what do we make of the second change from 2 Kings? Given the later date of Chronicles, could it be that the group behind these texts was less comfortable with a female prophet having any part of the last great Judahite ruler's effort to get the people of Judah back in right relationship with the Holy and with neighbor? Unfortunately, we will never know the reasons for this altering of the storyline, but we can still recognize other elements that point to Huldah's prestige and importance as prophet, priest, scribe, interpreter of texts, and canonizer of holy writ.

Huldah—A Childfree Woman

As Arlene Swidler has reminded us, Huldah's resume is quite impressive: "a prophet of stature, consultant to the high priest and king, and the founder of biblical criticism."[29] To these roles we can add wife, scribe, priest, canonizer, and reformer. The one role not found among Huldah's accomplishments is that of mother. Unlike her sister prophets Miriam and Deborah, Huldah is described as married, so motherhood could have been a possibility for her. Thus it is especially notable that this descriptor is completely absent in portrayals of her. There were many demands on her time and attention: being available for consultations with the king, with the high priest, or both; engaging in study and perhaps teaching; listening attentively for the Divine's inspiration; maintaining a relationship with her spouse; and completing other unnamed tasks. How could Huldah have had time to be pregnant and to nurse and raise children? According to the biblical texts, she did not. Her

29. Swidler, "In Search of Huldah," 1783.

69

calling was to other important roles in the life of the Jerusalem community and to sacred work.

Huldah serves as a role model for women today who are wondering if they have a place in a society that puts so much value on motherhood. While she may have been a token female in the male-dominated story of preexilic Judah, Huldah is not afraid to speak truth to power. Note that her words implicitly condemn Hilkiah the high priest and other members of King Josiah's envoy. It's possible that the Deuteronomistic History uses her to support its theological agenda, but Huldah still is part of the story. Even if her voice is employed to silence Asherah worship, there is no evidence that the worship of this female deity helped elevate women's status in ancient Israel. Huldah plays an important role that cannot be overshadowed by other prophets, like Jeremiah. We can hear in her words a call to faithfulness to the Holy One, for whom no one image is sufficient, and by whom we are commanded to love others as we love ourselves. Huldah's power to authenticate sacred texts empowers us to read biblical texts with a hermeneutic of suspicion and to claim what we find in Scripture to be true to our understanding of what it means to be a woman created in the image of the Divine.

I am Huldah . . .

I am a prophet, . . . but there is no book of Huldah.

I declared a text to be holy writ, . . . but there is no information about my education.

I advised a king, . . . but there is no mention of me among his entourage.

I told the people what they needed to hear, . . . but I receive no credit for my having inspired a reform.

I was labeled the weasel,[30] . . . but I dug for the truth of the text.

---

30. This is found in b. Meg. 14b. In Hebrew her name can mean "weasel."

6

ESTHER

Politician, Strategist, Cultic Leader, Sage, Prophet, & Savior

Introducing Esther

The book of Esther creates a picture of the Jewish diaspora. Under a foreign ruler, the Jews' faith is threatened, as well as their lives, by those who are prejudiced against them. On the verge of being victims of genocide, the Jews appear to have no control over the irreversible edict of the Persian king. Yet, hope is not lost. They have a court insider who is Jewish, Queen Esther. At another crisis point in the story of the Jewish people, a woman emerges as their savior. Like her foresisters, Queen Esther provides the wisdom, political savvy, and courage to remove the threat to her people. While some might critique the way Esther goes about this rescue, she uses whatever tools she has to defeat a male enemy. Esther undergoes a radical transformation from a passive character to a brave leader. Her skills of strategy and diplomacy are allowed to emerge so that she can rescue her people. Yet in the end Esther fades out of the biblical text, but not out of the people's memory.

The book of Esther is one of two biblical books named for a woman; the other is Ruth. If we include the Apocrypha, then there are two more: Judith and Susanna. Like the book of Ruth, Esther is a self-contained story that has captivated biblical readers through the centuries. The first aspect of

Esther that stands out is that it was almost left on the cutting room floor of the Jewish and Christian canons. For early Jewish leaders trying to identify a core group of authoritative texts, what would become the TaNaK, Esther was problematic for at least one clear reason; the Holy is never mentioned in the Hebrew manuscripts. There were also issues around the violence in the story and the possible pagan origins of Purim, the Jewish holiday that traces its roots to the book. Thankfully, the leaders recognized that there were other violent texts and pagan elements in other sacred texts and wisely decided to include Esther in the canon. Later, Christian theologians expressed their dislike of the book and even doubted it's canonicity; this doubt was voiced by Martin Luther: "I am so great an enemy to the second book of the Maccabees, and to Esther, that I wish they had not come to us at all, for they have too many heathen unnaturalities."[1]

Beyond general agreement that Esther qualifies as a narrative, there has been little consensus about the genre of the book. The descriptions of its genre run the gamut from farce to satire to Jewish novella. "Its far-fetched narrative features unlikely heroes and heroines, fools and fops, plodders and plotters, virgins and villains."[2] The book of Esther "is an imaginative story . . . it is a comedy, a book meant to be funny, to provoke laughter."[3] Adele Berlin goes on to highlight the "low comedy" of the story, including even burlesque elements. However, the subject matter of the book is very serious, dealing with matters of violence in general, genocide in particular, and the treatment of women by an androcentric environment. David J. Zucker considers it a "cautionary tale about the uses and abuses of power, and how one needs to be vigilant in a potentially hostile world."[4] Orlando E. Costas argues for seeing Esther and her story as a subversive story about liberation.[5]

The majority of biblical scholars do agree that Esther is fiction, perhaps historicized fiction with at least partial knowledge of the Persian court. The date of the book's composition, though, is hard to determine. Some argue that the book was written during the Persian period (in the fourth century BCE), which was a time of mostly peaceful coexistence between the Jewish

1. Luther, *The Table Talk of Martin Luther*, 24.
2. Zucker, "The Importance of Being Esther," 102.
3. Berlin, *Esther*, xvii.
4. Berlin, *Esther*, xvii.
5. Costas, "The Subversiveness of Faith," 67.

people and the government.[6] Others make a case for the book's dating to the Hellenistic period (the third century BCE),[7] or even to the time of the Maccabees (between 167 and 140 BCE)[8] but couched during the reign of a Persian king in order to call out the abuses of later Greek rulers.[9] Perhaps the best we can estimate is that the book's composition was no earlier than the Persian Empire (circa 486–465 BCE) and no later than the first extra-biblical evidence of the book of Esther (circa 70 CE).

The story of Esther is set within the Persian Empire, under the reign of King Ahaseurus (perhaps connected to Xerxes I) in the summer capital of Susa. Under the leadership of Cyrus, the Persians had defeated the Babylonians in 539 BCE, thus taking control of their empire, which included Israel/Palestine—known as Judea in the world of Esther. The general picture is that the Persians were less harsh in their treatment of the people in conquered lands. It was Cyrus who, in 538 BCE, issued an edict that allowed exiles in Babylon to return to their homelands, including those taken from Judah. However, not all of the exiles chose to return; some decided to remain in their new locations. It was under the Persian's control that Jerusalem was rebuilt, including the temple, and that the reconstructed Jewish community in Judea could worship as they saw fit.

With this recollection of Persian rule, it is difficult to make sense of the diasporic danger that is portrayed in the book of Esther. She and Mordecai are living in Susa and seem to face some prejudice simply for being Jewish. This seems incongruent with the relative freedom enjoyed in the Persian Empire. On the other hand, the story does portray the possibility of a Jewish woman becoming queen, as long as she hides that part of her identity.[10] Perhaps the backdrop for the story reflects a compilation of the more unpleasant rulers and experiences that the Jewish people had suffered not just under the Greeks but also later empires. Of course, the absolute authority of monarchs can always corrupt absolutely individual rulers, such as we see in the royal court of King Ahaseurus.

---

6. Niditch, "Legends of Wise Heroes and Heroines," 446.

7. Wills, *The Jewish Novel*, 96.

8. Niditch, "Legends," 445.

9. Stone, *Empire and Gender*, 15.

10. In fact, this is one of the reasons that some scholars argue that the story does not adequately reflect the Persian Empire because it would be unheard of for the queen to be not of a royal Persian line.

Esther has been the focus of much study by scholars who look at her through a feminist lens, and most find her extremely lacking. For many centuries, Mordecai has been celebrated as the main character and hero of the story, while Esther is simply a means to an end—the salvation of her people and Mordecai's rise to power in the Persian court. The discounting of Esther happens on multiple fronts, from her being a sex object to her using manipulation to get what she wants. Despite the fact that she risks her life to prevent Haman's genocidal desires, Esther is often maligned. One scholar states she is simply doing as she is told, while Mordecai "supplied the brains."[11] A feminist voice of the twentieth century summarizes her role in the story: "Esther comes in willingly to do what Vashti would not. Esther is, in effect, the scab undermining the impact of the striking worker's sacrifice."[12]

Plenty of scholars see more in Esther than just a "bimbo."[13] They have seen within her character a variety of positive roles, including as a liberator, as a wise advisor to the king, as a prophet, and so forth. One descriptor that does not get used in reference to Esther is the word *mother*. One characteristic of Esther does get connected directly to motherhood. Scholars who describe the wisdom of Esther and who draw parallels between her and other wise women in the Hebrew Bible assign the source of wisdom and authority to the domestic sphere, in particular to their assumed roles as mothers.[14] However, there is no indication from her story that Esther is a mother, so we might wonder if the culture acknowledged that besides from mothers, wisdom in a home might also come from aunts or other females without children. Or perhaps by the time the book of Esther was written down and disseminated, women were being educated so that their wisdom came from a public source. While feminist scholars have not tried to "motherize" Esther, they also don't draw attention to her childfree status. However, one male scholar recognizes the uniqueness of Esther as a female hero "whose importance to the Jewish people does not lie in childbearing."[15] Esther fulfills many roles in her story, but motherhood is definitely not one of them.

11. Moore, *Esther*, lii.

12. Duran, "Who Wants to Marry a Persian King?," 78.

13. Song, "Heartless Bimbo or Subversive Role Model?," 56–69.

14. Camp, "The Wise Women of 2 Samuel," 14.

15. Fox, "The Women in Esther."

Esther as a Savvy Politician—Esther 2:5–15

5 Now there was a Jew in the citadel of Susa whose name was Mordecai son of Jair son of Shimei son of Kish, a Benjaminite. 6 Kish had been carried away from Jerusalem among the captives carried away with King Jeconiah of Judah, whom King Nebuchadnezzar of Babylon had carried away. 7 Mordecai had brought up Hadassah, that is Esther, his cousin, for she had neither father nor mother; the girl was fair and beautiful, and when her father and her mother died, Mordecai adopted her as his own daughter. 8 So when the king's order and his edict were proclaimed, and when many young women were gathered in the citadel of Susa in custody of Hegai, Esther also was taken into the king's palace and put in custody of Hegai, who had charge of the women. 9 The girl pleased him and won his favor, and he quickly provided her with her cosmetic treatments and her portion of food, and with seven chosen maids from the king's palace, and advanced her and her maids to the best place in the harem. 10 Esther did not reveal her people or kindred, for Mordecai had charged her not to tell. 15 When the turn came for Esther daughter of Abihail the uncle of Mordecai, who had adopted her as his own daughter, to go in to the king, she asked for nothing except what Hegai the king's eunuch, who had charge of the women, advised. Now Esther was admired by all who saw her.

The character of Esther is a complex one. First, we learn that she actually has two names: Hadassah and Esther. The former is her Jewish name with a possible meaning of "myrtle," but her second name is probably her Persian name. Oddly enough, the name Esther is thought to be derived from the name of the goddess Istar.[16] Esther is an orphan of the second Babylonian deportation. Luckily, she is taken in by her cousin Mordecai. While most of her introduction in the story focuses on Mordecai and his lineage, we learn that Esther is "fair and beautiful" (Esth 2:7). Her life seems unremarkable beyond her appearance and her status as a "girl" (*na'arah*). However, when King Ahaseurus gets lonely after deposing Queen Vashti and decides to find a new mate, Esther's life changes dramatically. The king issues a call for all of the available "virgins" (*be'thulia*) to be brought to the royal harem in the "citadel of Susa" so that he might choose a new queen from among them. Esther too is taken to the harem and placed under the charge of Hegai, the king's eunuch, where she "pleased him and won his favor" (Esth 2:9). With Hegai on her side, she is given special attention in the

---

16. Similarly, Mordecai is traced to the god Marduk.

cosmetic treatments required of all the gathered women, and Hegai secures a prime placement for Esther and her maids. Having gained the admiration of all who encounter her, Esther's turn for a night with the king arrives. Ahaseurus is said to love her more than the other women; she achieves his "favor and devotion" and is immediately crowned queen. All of the kingdom celebrates her coronation and benefit from the king's happy generosity (Esth 2:16–18).

Many scholars, especially feminists, have identified Esther's passiveness and objectification in this first part of her story. Read with a hermeneutic of suspicion, it seems that Esther is the ideal woman: beautiful and passive. If we read the text with a recognition of its limits and those of the culture that produced it, what Susan Niditch refers to as "structured empathy," we might see more than what a twenty-first-century audience finds acceptable behavior. Yes, Esther is completely controlled by males, from Mordecai to Hegai to Ahaseurus. It's true that her voice is not heard, and she seems to have no choice in what her future will be. Esther has been accused of selling out to the male-dominated societal visions of femininity, to be seen and not heard. But what choice does she have? She is a subject of the king and property of her cousin. One did not disobey royal orders, at least not a young girl like Esther. She uses her body and her beauty to attain the prize of being queen, though that position could seem unappealing after what happened to Vashti and given the king's moodiness.

However, there are other ways to understand Esther's character in these opening scenes. Perhaps she is trying to make the best of a deplorable situation of being forced into a marriage and keeping her Jewish identity a secret, as Mordecai instructs her. Notice how she wins Hegai's "favor" and the admiration of everyone around her. In the first instance, the Hebrew word used is *hesed*, and the translation of "favor" does not do justice to this important Hebrew word. Often translated as "steadfast love," *hesed* is most often used in relation to the Divine. This is the kind of passionate love of the Holy that will not let go of people. The text also uses the Hebrew word *hen*, which means "grace" or "favor" and can also have the connotation of "acceptance." This word is often used in relation to seeking the "favor" or "grace" of the Divine. Surely this respect is not attained through Esther's physical beauty alone. Could it be that Esther is gaining skills at how to ingratiate herself to the right people? She is learning to be a savvy politician, making friends within the king's court, knowing that she might need those allies at some point in the future. That Esther listens to Hegai's advice about what to bring with her for her turn with the king shows that she actively seeks out advice on how to be a successful queen. As Angeline Song suggests, Esther is demonstrating the long-standing survival technique of oppressed people. "This may be described as a pragmatism of the powerless, where the disenfranchised survive by pleasing the people in power, making the best use of the opportunities offered by the system, cultivating the right allies and at all times by remaining humble and flexible."[17] Using what power she has and working within the system, Esther is working to attain a position of some authority, which one day will provide the opportunity to save the lives of her people.

Esther as Valuable Insider—Esther 2:16–18

16 When Esther was taken to King Ahasuerus in his royal palace in the tenth month, which is the month of Tebeth, in the seventh year of his reign, 17 the king loved Esther more than all the other women; of all the virgins she won his favor and devotion, so that he set the royal crown on her head and made her queen instead of Vashti. 18 Then the king gave a great banquet to all his officials and ministers—"Esther's banquet." He also granted a holiday to the provinces, and gave gifts with royal liberality.

The story is careful not to specifically describe what happens when one of the young women spends the night with the king and how she might "please" him, but the audience's imagination is quick to fill in the blanks. While it is implied, the text does not tell us that Esther had sex with Ahaseurus. What we do know is that he "loved" Esther and that she had won his *ḥen* (as she had among all who saw her) and *ḥesed*, as she had with Hegai. The king's strong reaction had to have been based on more than sex or beauty. Perhaps the king was impressed with Esther's diligence in overcoming the ordeal of months of preparation in order to meet him. He also may have found her a thoughtful woman, one who does her civic duty but in her own way. Did the king see an independent spark in Esther? He seemed to have a fondness for feisty women, if Vashti is any indication. Whatever it is that captures the king's heart, he is moved to crown Esther queen right in the moment. He puts the crown on her head, indicating that she is Vashti's replacement. The way the Hebrew describes this immediate coronation presents an intriguing translation possibility. The word translated as "made

17. Song, "Heartless Bimbo or Subversive Role Model," 60.

her queen" is the Hebrew word *mlk* which has the basic meaning of "rule" or "reign." However, the form of this verb used in Esth 2:17 is the hiphil, which carries with it an intensifying of the verb's basic meaning. A more wooden translation would say that "he caused her to reign," which may indicate that with the crown also came some authority in Ahasuerus's kingdom.[18] Esther has achieved insider status, which proves important later in the chapter, when she is able to prevent the assassination of the king by passing along Mordecai's discovery of the plot devised by two of Ahasuerus's eunuchs (Esth 2:19–22). "Overall, Esther is fast becoming a court insider despite the pressure of having to keep her racial identity a secret."[19]

Esther as an Emerging Leader—Esther 4:1–14

1 When Mordecai learned all that had been done, Mordecai tore his clothes and put on sackcloth and ashes, and went through the city, wailing with a loud and bitter cry; 2 he went up to the entrance of the king's gate, for no one might enter the king's gate clothed with sackcloth. 3 In every province, wherever the king's command and his decree came, there was great mourning among the Jews, with fasting and weeping and lamenting, and most of them lay in sackcloth and ashes. 4 When Esther's maids and her eunuchs came and told her, the queen was deeply distressed; she sent garments to clothe Mordecai, so that he might take off his sackcloth; but he would not accept them. 5 Then Esther called for Hathach, one of the king's eunuchs, who had been appointed to attend her, and ordered him to go to Mordecai to learn what was happening and why. 6 Hathach went out to Mordecai in the open square of the city in front of the king's gate, 7 and Mordecai told him all that had happened to him, and the exact sum of money that Haman had promised to pay into the king's treasuries for the destruction of the Jews. 8 Mordecai also gave him a copy of the written decree issued in Susa for their destruction, that he might show it to Esther, explain it to her, and charge her to go to the king to make supplication to him and entreat him for her people. 9 Hathach went and told Esther what Mordecai had said. 10 Then Esther spoke to Hathach and gave him a message for Mordecai, saying, 11 "All the king's servants and the people of the king's provinces know that if any man or woman goes to the king inside the inner court without being called, there is but one law—all alike are

18. Hancock, "Esther and the Politics of Negotiation," 140.

19. Song, "Heartless Bimbo or Subversive Role Model," 60.

to be put to death. Only if the king holds out the golden scepter to someone, may that person live. I myself have not been called to come in to the king for thirty days." 12 When they told Mordecai what Esther had said, 13 Mordecai told them to reply to Esther, "Do not think that in the king's palace you will escape any more than all the other Jews. 14 For if you keep silence at such a time as this, relief and deliverance will rise for the Jews from another quarter, but you and your father's family will perish. Who knows? Perhaps you have come to royal dignity for just such a time as this."

In the intervening chapter, Mordecai and Haman, the king's right-hand man, have clashed. Haman expects Mordecai to bow before him as the king had ordered, but Mordecai refuses. This infuriates Haman, so he bribes Ahaseurus into signing an edict ordering the slaughter of all the Jews living in his kingdom. He states that the Jews' laws are contrary to those of the king, and he offers ten thousand talents of silver to be added to Ahaseurus's treasury. The king agrees and allows Haman to write the edict and issue it with the royal stamp. With Mordecai out of the way, Haman and Ahaseurus have a quiet evening meal. However, outside the palace there is great confusion and anxiety. Some of it is incited by Mordecai, who tears his clothes and goes throughout the city in sackcloth and ashes, loudly lamenting (along with the other Jews living in the Persian Empire) the fate that is to befall his people.

Powerless to change the edict, Mordecai brings his mourning to the palace gate and catches the attention of Esther's attendants. When the queen hears about Mordecai's behavior, she sends clothing to him in hopes that he might make himself more presentable. It is important to note that Esther seems to have no knowledge of Haman's plan to kill her people, partially because her identity as a Jew still remains a secret to the king and everyone else in the palace. After Mordecai refuses the clothing, she sends Hathach, one of the King's eunuchs, to discover what is the cause of Mordecai's troubling behavior. When Hathach returns with a copy of the edict and instructions from Mordecai for the queen to do something, Esther is greatly distressed. She responds that to enter the King's presence without an invitation would mean her death, or at least she would lose the crown. Mordecai reminds her that she will not be spared once people have learned that she is also a Jew, and he suggests that her ascent to the throne may have been providential, so that she might save her people from genocide.

This chapter is often identified as the turning point in Esther's character development.[20] Having been an obedient cousin and citizen, Esther has always done what her superiors have commanded. However, things have changed. Mordecai no longer has control over her actions. She is the queen, and she is concerned for the well-being of the kingdom. This is why she tries to change Mordecai's rather unseemly behavior. It is important to note that Esther does not go to Mordecai; she sends her servants to communicate with him because this is how royals interact with their subjects. Esther knows that no decision should be made without gathering as much information as possible, so she sends the eunuch to learn the cause of Mordecai's lament. Only after learning about the edict to destroy the Jews can Esther get the full picture of what is happening in the kingdom.

Many have critiqued Esther's original resistance to Mordecai's order that she do something to save her people as cowardly or uncaring.[21] However, it seems more likely that this is an example of her wisdom and emerging political leadership. "Esther's first reaction is that of an intelligent politician, one who knows the consequences of violating court etiquette. She is reluctant to risk her own life and position for a cause that may well be lost no matter what she says, or that, judging from Vashti's fate, she may well never get to plead."[22] If Esther is to take action, it has to be done with care and tact, abiding by the laws of Ahaseurus. "As a woman in a very male-dominated, patriarchal world, she has to be very careful about what she does or does not do, much less in for what she seeks to achieve."[23] Whether or not her being chosen as queen is providential, what Mordecai asks of Esther is overwhelmingly dangerous and somewhat unfair. Having been the one to advise her not to let anyone in the palace know she is Jewish, he is now asking her to reveal that part of her identity at the very moment that such an affiliation could mean she also will be slaughtered. In many ways, this is a no-win situation; however, Esther decides to take action and try to save her people.

---

20. See, for example, Fox, "The Women in Esther." Fox describes the acts of Esther that "foreshadow her role as a national leader: she sends, she commands, she inquires," 6 .

21. This is often found in Sunday school and devotional materials. For example, Deffinbaugh, "3. Esther's Dilemma and Decision"; and Lubitch "A Feminist's Look at Esther."

22. Bronner, "Reclaiming Esther," 6.

23. Zucker, "Entertaining Esther," 6.

Esther as Religious Leader—4:15–17

15 Then Esther said in reply to Mordecai, 16 "Go, gather all the Jews to be found in Susa, and hold a fast on my behalf, and neither eat nor drink for three days, night or day. I and my maids will also fast as you do. After that I will go to the king, though it is against the law; and if I perish, I perish." 17 Mordecai then went away and did everything as Esther had ordered him.

Once Esther decides to risk her life and go before the king without an invitation, her transformation mentioned above is manifested in her next words and actions. She commands Mordecai to have all the Jews in Susa hold a fast on her behalf for three days and three nights. The imperative verbs used here are an indication of this change in Esther from a controlled object to an empowered woman. She is now telling Mordecai what to do, and Queen Esther takes center stage. She has become "a shrewd and sapient queen with much agency."[24] In the face of such a great crisis, Esther makes an informed decision to engage in what essentially translates to civil disobedience. Like those before her, including Shiprah and Puah (the Israelite midwives who disobeyed Pharaoh and spared male Israelite babies before the exodus [Exod 1:15–21]) and Rizpah (one of King Saul's concubines, who honored the bodies of Saul's sons murdered by David [2 Sam 21:10–14]), Esther stands against an unjust and murderous political pogrom. And like Moses and Miriam before her, Esther is now tasked with the liberation of her people. In declaring a fast for all Jews, "Esther is assuming the role of a religious and national leader."[25]

Although the absence of any reference to the Holy in the book of Esther has caused many readers to dismiss the book as more secular than sacred, there is not a complete lack of religiosity in the book. Esther's request for a fast seems to indicate that she understands some of the Jewish rituals and even practices them herself, as Esth 4:16b indicates. Throughout the Hebrew Bible, fasting is a very common religious practice. "Moreover, because prayer frequently accompanies fasting in the Hebrew Bible, Esther's command may well have been understood to include prayer for God's intercession."[26] Leila Bronner also points out how this order of Esther is the direct opposite of all the feasting that has been described up to this point

---

24. Song, "Heartless Bimbo or Subversive Role Model?," 62.

25. Fox, "The Women in Esther."

26. Bronner, "Reclaiming Esther," 7.

in the story. Thus, "Esther's declaration of and participation in a fast is an astonishingly explicit announcement of faith."[27]

Even if this implicit religious act is not accepted as proof of Esther's religiosity, there can be another way of understanding the lack of reference to the Divine in the book of Esther. The idea of human inspiration and action being the way that the Holy shows up in the story is not original to Esther. In Genesis, we see how the character of the Divine becomes less and less directly engaged in the action of the ancestral stories. From a Being who walks and talks with humans in the opening chapters of Genesis (as well as in the stories around the ancestors), the Holy becomes merely an assumed presence in the story of Joseph. Clearly there is an understanding in the concluding chapters of Genesis of the Divine orchestrating the events that take place in Joseph's life, but there is no direct Divine intervention into the story. Could not the same be said about book of Esther? There are a few hints at Divine providence playing a part in Esther's rise to the throne as queen. Some have suggested that given the apparent silence of the Divine in the texts, Esther must draw her strength from the Jewish community. It is not unusual in the Hebrew Bible to see the Holy showing up in the collective of the faithful. "When all else fails, Esther depends with boundless confidence on the divine energy generated by communal fasting and prayer."[28]

Esther as Brilliant Strategist, Sage, and Prophet
—Esther 5:1–7 and 7:1–6

1 On the third day Esther put on her royal robes and stood in the inner court of the king's palace, opposite the king's hall. The king was sitting on his royal throne inside the palace opposite the entrance to the palace. 2 As soon as the king saw Queen Esther standing in the court, she won his favor and he held out to her the golden scepter that was in his hand. Then Esther approached and touched the top of the scepter. 3 The king said to her, "What is it, Queen Esther? What is your request? It shall be given you, even to the half of my kingdom." 4 Then Esther said, "If it pleases the king, let the king and Haman come today to a banquet that I have prepared for the king." 5 Then the king said, "Bring Haman quickly, so that we may do as Esther desires." So the king and Haman came to the banquet that Esther had prepared. 6 While they were drinking

27. Bronner, "Reclaiming Esther," 6–7.
28. Jackowski, "Holy Disobedience," 405.

wine, the king said to Esther, "What is your petition? It shall be granted you. And what is your request? Even to the half of my kingdom, it shall be fulfilled." 7 Then Esther said, "This is my petition and request: 8 If I have won the king's favor, and if it pleases the king to grant my petition and fulfill my request, let the king and Haman come tomorrow to the banquet that I will prepare for them, and then I will do as the king has said."

1 So the king and Haman went in to feast with Queen Esther. 2 On the second day, as they were drinking wine, the king again said to Esther, "What is your petition, Queen Esther? It shall be granted you. And what is your request? Even to the half of my kingdom, it shall be fulfilled." 3 Then Queen Esther answered, "If I have won your favor, O king, and if it pleases the king, let my life be given me—that is my petition—and the lives of my people—that is my request. 4 For we have been sold, I and my people, to be destroyed, to be killed, and to be annihilated. If we had been sold merely as slaves, men and women, I would have held my peace; but no enemy can compensate for this damage to the king." 5 Then King Ahasuerus said to Queen Esther, "Who is he, and where is he, who has presumed to do this?" 6 Esther said, "A foe and enemy, this wicked Haman!"

After the three-day fast is over, Esther is now all alone and must rely on her intelligence and knowledge of the king to create a strategy for saving her people. The text does not indicate that anyone advised her on what to do. The first step requires her to face the dangers of going before the king uninvited. Her concern is not unfounded. After all, Ahasuerus had dismissed Vashti for disobeying his command. She wisely dons her royal garments; she must remind the king and his court that she is the queen. Esther does not directly go before the king; rather, she positions herself where she might capture her husband's attention. Given the description of how Ahasuerus first responds to Esther, it is not surprising that when he sees her, she "wins his favor" again. By extending the royal scepter, he invites his wife to stand before him and speak.

While some might expect that Esther would make her plea before the throne to save the Jewish people, she invites the king and Haman to a banquet in her quarters. Esther realizes that this is not the time or the place to make such a daring request even if Ahasuerus has offered her half of his kingdom. Instead, Esther's plan is to remove both the king and Haman from the arena of their power and to bring them into her space. This more circuitous approach puts her in a position of power and provides an opportunity for her to butter up the king and lure Haman into complacency. Both men are quick to accept the invitation, and Ahaseurus once again offers Esther half of his kingdom. Still, Esther does not ask for what she really wants, but she invites the two men to another banquet on the next day. Like bread that is not yet ready to be taken from the oven, Esther's plan still needs some work.

Her inclusion of Haman in the banquet invitations has accomplished one of her goals; he is feeling very proud and brags about his favored status. After Esther has wined and dined them a second time, the king again offers to grant anything Esther desires. The queen discerns that this is the moment to make her move; however, she does not simply ask the king to save the Jewish people. Esther couches her request in well-chosen words: rhetoric intended to be humble and at the same time to incite the king's anger. "She begins on a familiar note of humility and then cuts to the chase."[29] Completely confident in Ahaseurus's devotion to her, Esther reveals that an order has been given for her people to be killed, endangering even her own life. Distraught about the potential loss of his wife, he asks her about the source of this threat. Finally, the moment of revelation has come, and she points to the unsuspecting Haman. In order to protect her husband from sharing in the blame for Haman's evil plot (though he had signed the edict), "Esther subtly makes the king out to be a joint victim together with her people, facing a common enemy."[30]

Esther's strategy works because of her "accurate, intelligent, politic assessment of the King's likely reactions."[31] Infuriated by this revelation, the king goes out to get some air and clear his head, leaving Esther and Haman alone (Esth 7:7). Realizing his vulnerability and recognizing that Esther has all the power, Haman throws himself at her mercy and begs for forgiveness. The king returns and sees Haman in a position that he interprets as threatening to Esther. This further enrages Ahaseurus, and Haman's fate is settled (Esth 7:8). Haman is killed using the very gallows that Haman had designed for Mordecai's death (Esth 5:14, 7:9–10). Part of Esther's request is fulfilled, but there is still the matter of the edict allowing for the Jewish people to be slaughtered. Haman had been the root of the impending violence, but his plan still lives.

29. Song, "Heartless Bimbo or Subversive Role Model?," 65.
30. Song, "Heartless Bimbo or Subversive Role Model?," 65.
31. Bronner, "Reclaiming Esther," 7.

In this scene, we see Esther's gifts of strategizing and wisdom. All the steps she takes are sagaciously chosen. Comparisons have been made between Esther and the wise women found in 2 Samuel, especially the wise woman of Tekoa (2 Sam 14). Both Esther and the wise woman of Tekoa "dress in a particular way in order to act out the persuasive drama."[32] The wise woman of Tekoa tells a story to King David in hopes that it will inspire him to forgive his son. She creates the opportunity for the king to see what the just action is, before he realizes what this will require of him. Like her and other biblical women, Esther is "so persuasive precisely because she makes the situation personal, providing a psychological motivation for responding to her request."[33] Leila Bronner describes Esther as a "sage," embodying wisdom and successfully maneuvering within the constraints of a patriarchal society and the Persian court milieu.[34]

The connection between Esther and the wise woman of Tekoa allows us to consider another of Esther's roles in this part of the story, that of prophet. One way of understanding the role of prophet is as one who subverts the status quo, refusing to "accept a negative event as fate or an accident of history . . . [identifying] a wicked historical deed and [challenging] it in the name of justice."[35] Like both the wise woman of Tekoa and Nathan (prophet of David), Esther must address a flaw in the structures of power that have been created by those in positions of authority. All three must remind a king that the violence they have supported is an inappropriate use of their power.[36] These prophets take the approach of softening up the one who must be confronted in order to elicit the desired response. Esther's entire strategy sets up "a situation in which the king almost cannot refuse her; like the woman of Tekoa and Nathan, she has almost guaranteed the response before the king even realizes how it implicates him."[37]

As a prophet, Esther faces a challenge similar to the challenges faced by others who came before; speaking truth to power is no easy task. Parallels have also been drawn between her and Moses. Both must enter the court of a foreign ruler and convince that ruler to liberate their people (Moses from slavery, Esther from certain death). Esther even has a call scene typical of

32. Hancock, "Esther and the Politics of Negotiation," 73.

33. Hancock, "Esther and the Politics of Negotiation," 95.

34. Bronner, "Reclaiming Esther," 4, 8.

35. Costas, "The Subversiveness of Faith," 66.

36. Bronner, "Reclaiming Esther," 7.

37. Hancock, "Esther and the Politics of Negotiation," 95.

most of the biblical prophets. It has four basic parts: a call from the Divine, a description of the mission, a refusal by the person called, and some assurance from the Divine that the called person can do what is needed. Esther's call and mission come through the mouth of Mordecai (but may be assumed to originate with the Holy), and she does give an excuse for why she can't do this (the edict against going before the king uninvited). Mordecai's famous phrase about her being in her current position of influence for a time like this could be understood as a reassurance, but Esther never gets a sign or a true Divine affirmation. Instead, she is left to her own skills and intellect to figure out how to carry out this mission. Luckily for Esther, her call is fulfilled without much cost to her, and her mission is more successful than those of other prophets. Perhaps, we could see her as one of the true prophets whose impassioned pleas actually convince their audience to change their behavior.

Esther as Savior of Her People—Esther 8:1–8

1 On that day King Ahasuerus gave to Queen Esther the house of Haman, the enemy of the Jews; and Mordecai came before the king, for Esther had told what he was to her. 2 Then the king took off his signet ring, which he had taken from Haman, and gave it to Mordecai. So Esther set Mordecai over the house of Haman. 3 Then Esther spoke again to the king; she fell at his feet, weeping and pleading with him to avert the evil design of Haman the Agagite and the plot that he had devised against the Jews. 4 The king held out the golden scepter to Esther, 5 and Esther rose and stood before the king. She said, "If it pleases the king, and if I have won his favor, and if the thing seems right before the king, and I have his approval, let an order be written to revoke the letters devised by Haman son of Hammedatha the Agagite, which he wrote giving orders to destroy the Jews who are in all the provinces of the king. 6 For how can I bear to see the calamity that is coming on my people? Or how can I bear to see the destruction of my kindred?" 7 Then King Ahasuerus said to Queen Esther and to the Jew Mordecai, "See, I have given Esther the house of Haman, and they have hanged him on the gallows, because he plotted to lay hands on the Jews. 8 You may write as you please with regard to the Jews, in the name of the king, and seal it with the king's ring; for an edict written in the name of the king and sealed with the king's ring cannot be revoked."

With Haman out of the way, the king gives Esther Haman's house and signet ring. She makes Mordecai the overseer of the property and gives him
the ring, making Mordecai the king's new advisor. Esther has essentially or-
chestrated a coup, turning the tables so that she and Mordecai take the position that Haman had so desired.[38] Ahasuerus thinks everything is settled,
but this is not the justice that Esther is seeking. She has not been striving for
power or her own safety; her mission is greater. There is still the problem of
the original edict that ordered the genocide of the Jewish people. Since we
had learned earlier in the story that an official edict cannot be canceled or
undone (Esth 1:19), Esther has another plan to save her people. With the
same language of humility and emotion, she continues her strategy to play
upon the king's love for her in order to get what she wants. Esther requests
that the king issue another edict that would allow the Jews to defend themselves against those who seek to annihilate them. Ahasuerus gives free rein
to Esther and Mordecai to write whatever they desire in his name and to
seal it with his ring (Esth 8:7–8). So, they issue an edict (written in every
language of the kingdom) declaring that on the thirtieth day of Adar the
Jews should be ready to destroy their enemies (Esth 8:9–14). This news is
received by the Jewish community with celebration (Esth 8:16).

Esther as Cultic Official and Queen—Esther 9:25–32

25 but when Esther came before the king, he gave orders in writing that the wicked plot that he had devised against the Jews
should come upon his own head, and that he and his sons should
be hanged on the gallows. 26 Therefore these days are called Purim, from the word Pur. Thus because of all that was written in
this letter, and of what they had faced in this matter, and of what
had happened to them, 27 the Jews established and accepted as a
custom for themselves and their descendants and all who joined
them, that without fail they would continue to observe these two
days every year, as it was written and at the time appointed. 28
These days should be remembered and kept throughout every
generation, in every family, province, and city; and these days of
Purim should never fall into disuse among the Jews, nor should
the commemoration of these days cease among their descendants.
29 Queen Esther daughter of Abihail, along with the Jew Mordecai, gave full written authority, confirming this second letter about
Purim. 30 Letters were sent wishing peace and security to all the

38. Bronner, "Reclaiming Esther," 8.

Jews, to the one hundred twenty-seven provinces of the kingdom of Ahasuerus, 31 and giving orders that these days of Purim should be observed at their appointed seasons, as the Jew Mordecai and Queen Esther enjoined on the Jews, just as they had laid down for themselves and for their descendants regulations concerning their fasts and their lamentations. 32 The command of Queen Esther fixed these practices of Purim, and it was recorded in writing.

Esther has now saved her people from genocide. Her next act is to establish a holiday to commemorate the thwarting of the abusive power and the many ways the Jewish people worked together for this common goal. While the text implies that Mordecai is the source for the first letter, it is Esther who writes the second. As queen she declares an annual two-day festival, called Purim, and names the rituals (lamentations and fasts) for how to observe this religious holiday. Here again we see Esther taking on the role of religious leader for the Jews in the Persian kingdom. Like the fast she declares in the third chapter, these practices imply a Divine element even without the actual naming of the Holy. The festival is not celebrating Esther but rather Divine providence that lies behind all that had transpired so that the Jewish people continued.

Queen Esther sends her letters wishing "peace and security" to all her people. The NRSV translation does not quite reflect the fullness of what she wanted for the Jews. The word rendered as "peace" is the Hebrew word *shalom*, which has a more appropriate definition as "wholeness," not the lack of conflict. Likewise, the word translated as "security" is the Hebrew word *'emet* that has a more accurate sense of "faithfulness" and "truth." Esther is not sending an assurance that the people are no longer in danger, but a prayer that they will find a completeness and remain strong in their faith. It sounds like the letter of a clergy person more than that of a queen.

The idea of Esther as a cultic leader is not often discussed, but certainly establishing a religious and national holiday would be within the purview of a priest. Is it possible that as queen, Esther was a priest of a female deity? There have been some connections made between Esther and the goddess Ishtar (beyond just her name). "Purim's origins, scholars generally agree, derive from an ancient full-moon pre-spring Persian holiday."[39] Ishtar is understood as the ruler of the morning and evening stars, and Esther's Hebrew name, Hadassah, can have the meaning of "myrtle, which has

39. Schnur, "The Womantasch Triangle."

star-shaped flowers."[40] While monotheism was the requirement of Judaism, it was not unusual for religious syncretism to emerge, when the people were under a foreign power. While those who included the book of Esther in the canon probably did not embrace this trend, it is possible that the story of Esther/Hadassah reveals the common ancient Near Eastern practice for a queen to be the priest of a female deity.[41] Since there is no mention of the Divine in the story, it is also possible to imagine that the deity Esther represented was still the God of Israel, which had no distinct sex or gender.

Esther—A Childfree Woman

The character of Esther has been much maligned by biblical scholars throughout the ages and has been tamed by others. However, some of those critiques have reflected more about the interpreter than the text. In a close reading of the story, Esther emerges as more than a pretty face. She acts as a savvy politician, a cultic leader, a gifted strategist, a prophet, a sage, and a savior of her people—all the while developing into an impressive queen. Her role in the story of the Jewish people was valued enough to receive canonical status. Like women before and after her, Esther worked within an oppressive system that sought to limit the power of outsiders (including women) and found a way to bring salvation for her people. None of her actions is deceptive, although she only reveals the whole truth at the right time. This is often a practice of the oppressed, who must use whatever power they have to compensate for the authority they lack.

While many have sung Vashti's praises as the true hero of the story of Esther, one must wonder what would have happened had Esther followed her path. Esther might have stood for her principles, but she would have lost the position that allowed her to subvert the genocidal desires of Haman. "In military terms, Vashti won the battle, but she helped lose the war. Male domination in Persia was ultimately strengthened and not weakened by Vashti's action."[42] It was left to Esther to use the male domination to her advantage, subverting the system. "Being shrewd, pragmatic and patient may be much more useful in the long term than a fruitless act of overt

40. Schnur, "The Womantasch Triangle."

41. For more information about the role of queens as priests of female deities, see Ackerman, "The Queen Mother."

42. Song, "Heartless Bimbo or Subversive Role Model?," 60.

disobedience . . . Esther shows how beauty, brains and wisdom need not be mutually exclusive."[43]

Among the multiple dimensions of the character Esther, one is obviously absent for the well-versed biblical reader. Esther is never described as a mother or as barren. She is a childfree woman who expands the roles of women beyond their reproductive capabilities. While some might argue that she could have birthed children later in life, that is not relevant to the current study. What is important is that given the Hebrew Bible's heavy emphasis on fertility as the primary role for females, there is an entire book about a woman who saved her people not by producing the right son but by using her intellect and courage to stop the genocide of the Jews.

I am Esther . . .

I was a Jewish orphan girl, . . . but I became a Persian queen.

I was told what to do by my uncle, . . . but I ruled over the land.

I was caught in a male game of power, . . . but I had the final word.

I was warned to hide my Jewish identity, . . . but I became the savior
of my people.

I have been judged for using my beauty, . . . but I also used my intellect.

I have been overshadowed by Mordecai, . . . but I am a part of the story.

---

43. Song, "Heartless Bimbo or Subversive Role Model?," 67.

7

OTHER WOMEN

A Medium and Wise Women

There are three unnamed women in the Hebrew Bible who are never identified as mothers or as barren, and they are portrayed as fulfilling roles that would have been understood in the ancient Near East as ritual expert, sage, and prophet. These three women are also presented without any connection to males, thus making them free agents, so to speak. That is, they are neither controlled by men (e.g., by father, husband, brothers, or sons) nor confined by the demands of childbearing and care. Though the texts provide them no names, a considerable amount of words is attributed to these three female characters; each of whom is given a voice and granted some authority by the other characters in their stories. While there is much unknown about these women, from their stories one can still glean insights about possible roles filled by (reserved for?) childfree women.

Introducing the Medium of Endor

Despite the fact that the religion portrayed in the Hebrew Bible presents a very negative view of magic and sorcery, the repetitive admonitions against such practices indicate that they were never truly absent from the Israelite culture. There are laws found within the texts that condemn such practices (e.g., Exod 22:18; Lev 19:26, 31; 20:27; Deut 18:10–11); some even state the punishment for engaging in these activities as death. This so-called magic is seen as foreign to the worship of YHWH, as something that other religions embraced but as outside the boundaries of acceptable Israelite religion. There is ample evidence that magic and access to the supernatural was prevalent throughout the ancient Near East, and it would be illogical to assume that these same interests and behaviors did not find a place in Israelite life.

Of interest for this examination is the strong opposition to necromancy,[1] with stoning as the consequence for anyone practicing such magic. However, there is one instance where neither the art of necromancy nor the practitioner is explicitly condemned, and this is in the story about the medium of Endor. In fact, the portrayal of the female in I Sam 28 is surprisingly positive. Not only is she able to grant the disguised king's request, but she also provides Saul with sustenance after the trauma he experiences from Samuel's strong rebuke.

Shrewd Professional Woman—1 Samuel 28:7–10

7 Then Saul said to his servants, "Seek out for me a woman who is a medium, so that I may go to her and inquire of her." His servants said to him, "There is a medium at Endor." 8 So Saul disguised himself and put on other clothes and went there, he and two men with him. They came to the woman by night. And he said, "Consult a spirit for me, and bring up for me the one whom I name to you." 9 The woman said to him, "Surely you know what Saul has done, how he has cut off the mediums and the wizards from the land. Why then are you laying a snare for my life to bring about my death?" 10 But Saul swore to her by the Lord, "As the Lord lives, no punishment shall come upon you for this thing."

The renown of the medium of Endor seems obvious by the fact that when Saul commands his servants to "seek out for me a woman who is a medium," they quickly respond that there is such a practitioner in Endor. They did not have to look it up in a phonebook or ask around; the location and vocation of the woman is readily known. Given the opening statement about how Saul had erased all who practiced magic from the land, it is even more striking that this woman's existence and location are so readily known. Clearly, the Israelites still need such professionals to help them in their daily lives; however, it is one thing for a common citizen (or even a

1. Necromancy is the practice of communicating with the dead.

servant or slave) to be a customer of a medium, but for the king who out-lawed such practices to seek her services displays not only his desperation but also his own recognition that such an edict would not end such necessary and popular practices. Because of his position, Saul must disguise himself in order not to be seen at such an establishment. Traveling under cover of darkness aids his secrecy, and nighttime is probably a good time for calling up the dead.

The woman's response to Saul's request is ironic. Afraid of being a victim of entrapment, she cites the law that Saul had instituted back to the disguised king. She asks this stranger if he has not heard about how the king had "cut off the mediums and the wizards from the land" (v. 9b). Her response, when compared to the preceding statement that "Saul had ex-pelled the mediums and the wizards from the land" (v. 3b), seems to intensify the king's actions. "Although we are told in v. 3 that Saul has removed (cha'sir) the sorcerers, the witch says that Saul has cut them off (karat). Unlike modern literary stylists, the biblical author does not vary words merely to avoid repetition. We are meant to notice that the witch uses a more lethal verb than does the narrator."[2] Her use of this verb, "cut off," can be seen as referring to the death sentence waiting for any "sorcerer"; however, it also makes the impact of Saul's act even more powerful. It's not just a religious ban; it has also "cut off" the woman's means of supporting herself. In other words, Saul is her enemy, who has attempted to end her livelihood and her life. If she grants the request of her nocturnal visitor, she is in grave danger. Saul assures her that she will not be punished, but is that a real promise? There are too many instances of women being blamed for the misdeeds of men or being left holding the bag while men disappear. Even with this promise, what the woman does next is risky.[3]

The title given to this woman has provided fodder for many scholarly considerations. The phrase in Hebrew, 'eshet ba'alat 'ov, is difficult to translate because of the unique construction. The first word, 'eshet, is the very common noun 'ishah (translated as either "woman" or "wife"[4]) in

---

2. Reis, "Eating the Blood," 8.

3. Fischer, in "1 Samuel 28" suggests that this opening exchange "may be part of a ritual to set the medium free and to guarantee magical protection" (32). Only then can the consultation take place.

4. In Hebrew there is no separate word for "wife," so the noun, 'ishah, which has the basic meaning of "woman" is often translated as "wife" based on context. However, it is important to note that the lack of a separate word for "wife" may indicate the societal/linguistic constraints placed on women in the culture behind the stories. To be a woman

the construct form, denoting its relationship to the following words. The phrase *ba'alat 'ov*, is more difficult to translate given the lack of parallels throughout the Hebrew Bible. The first noun, *ba'alat*, is also in its construct form and typically translated as "mistress of," as in "mistress of the house." In more contemporary language, as an attempt to prevent the normal negative associations with "mistress," it might be rendered as "manager" or "specialist" or "expert." The final word of the construct chain, *'ov*, has the basic meanings of "skin bottle" and "spirit" or "ghost." There have been suggestions that this word is connected to the Hebrew word *'ab*, meaning "father" or "ancestor" and may connect to the concept of deceased ancestors that a specialist can contact on behalf of the living.[5] The woman's title could be rendered as a female specialist of spirits. This phrase *'eshet ba'alat 'ov* is not found anywhere else in the Hebrew Bible, "but the implication is that, at least within the world of the story, it is a recognized role."[6]

Ritual Expert—1 Samuel 28:11–14

11 Then the woman said, "Whom shall I bring up for you?" He answered, "Bring up Samuel for me." 12 When the woman saw Samuel, she cried out with a loud voice; and the woman said to Saul, "Why have you deceived me? You are Saul!" 13 The king said to her, "Have no fear; what do you see?" The woman said to Saul, "I see a divine being coming up out of the ground." 14 He said to her, "What is his appearance?" She said, "An old man is coming up; he is wrapped in a robe." So Saul knew that it was Samuel, and he bowed with his face to the ground, and did obeisance.

When this female character is defined as a "witch," the implicit message is that she is evil, one who works against the Divine. Surely, she could not be described as a ritual expert unless that is set within a foreign or pagan context. In fact, many scholars have assumed that the woman is not Israelite and therefore has no real power. Despite the evidence in the text of the efficacy of her actions, some would have us believe that Samuel's appearance is controlled by the Holy and not by her. Esther Fuchs, for example, makes

---

was by definition to be a wife even if the female in question is never connected to a male.

5. Miller, "The Witch at the Navel of the World," 98. See also Fischer, "1 Samuel 28."

6. Hamori, *Women's Divination*, 105–6. Hamori concludes that this woman is not a sorceress or witch because the Hebrew word for those practices, *mkshph*, is not used. Instead, Hamori decides to use the phrase "ghost-diviner" for the woman's role (along with "medium" and "necromancer").

the claim that the medium "is no match for God's prophet,"[7] and Pamela Tamarkin Reis declares that Samuel "allowed himself to be raised" because of his close relationship with Saul.[8] Each of these scholars, along with others, seem to be attempting to deny the woman's authority over the deceased, perhaps out of a personal rejection of this ancient concept of raising the dead. However, without such twenty-first-century lenses, the role that the medium fulfills has parallels both within the authorized religion of Israel and the broader religious context of the ancient Near East.

One image that emerges from the identification of this woman's profession and practice is that of shaman, a title not typically associated with Israelite religious institutions. A shaman is often understood as one who can communicate with the spirits in order to answer questions posed to the shaman. Writing about shamans, J. P. Brown notes that one characteristic of shamans is that they are often seen as "handicapped" or "different."[9] In the case of the Hebrew Bible, one might make the case that being female was a handicap that prevented a person from being included in the official category of religious leadership. Given the recurring condemnation of magic (and especially necromancy), it seems that early religious traditions in Israel did embrace such practices. With the institution of a national religion and the priesthood in Israel, these early beliefs were either appropriated or denounced. In the case of magic, such rituals would have been conducted by the all-male priesthood, thereby eliminating the roles of the females who had originally presided. Meanwhile, male religious leaders "could and did perform some magical tasks within the framework of accepted religion."[10]

Another point of interest is the comingling of the medium's role and that of a prophet. Although the text describes a conversation between Samuel and Saul, one is left wondering how they communicated. Since the medium must describe Samuel for Saul, it appears that he could not see the conjured dead prophet. Then how is it that he can hear Samuel's words? Is it that she must also serve as the conduit of Samuel's words? This role could make her a prophet or at least the "harbinger of the prophetic

7. Fuchs, "Prophecy and the Construction of Women," 56.

8. Reis, "Eating the Blood," 9–10.

9. Brown, "The Mediterranean Seer and Shamanism," 377.

10. Brenner-Idan, *The Israelite Woman*, 71. Brenner-Idan identifies some magical rituals officiated by priests: the red heifer ceremony (Num 19), the goat of Azazel (Lev 16); and Moses's creation of the bronze serpent as a healing agent (Num 21).

word."[11] In fact, Susan Pigott makes the case that there is evidence within the text to support the woman's prophetic role. She identifies these two possible parallels: "the structure of the story and the terms used to describe Saul's encounter with the woman resemble the structure and terms used in later narratives describing prophetic consultation."[12] J. Lust identified the structure of these consultations as having these parts, along with their corresponding verses in 1 Sam 28: "War is at hand, the main character goes to the medium/prophet for guidance, and an answer foretelling future events is given. In this story, war is imminent (vv. 4–5); Saul goes to a medium (vv. 7–8) for guidance (v. 15); an answer is given by a prophet (vv. 16–19)."[13]

In continuing this linkage to prophecy, Esther Hamori notes that there are only two instances within the Deuteronomistic History where a king consults a female diviner: the current case of Saul and the medium and the later story of Josiah and Huldah. By labeling both female characters as "diviners," she makes the case that both women play very similar roles in their stories. "The comparison exposes a surprising lack of interest in the legitimacy of the divination and the diviner in each text."[14] Both women provide the king with access to a Divine word about the current state of affairs and the probable future outcome. While one might be enticed to condemn the medium and applaud the prophet, these texts do not sustain such a separation. Instead, they reveal that while necromancy might have been pushed a bit further away from the Holy than prophecy, this "is a matter of degree, not of kind."[15]

It is interesting that 1 Sam 28 does not provide information about how the woman performs the ritual that brings up Samuel from the dead. Perhaps this gap is due to the writers' lack of knowledge about necromancy, or it could be an intentional omission so as not to give any recognition to the skills of the medium. It might also be that because the details are missing, the story's emphasis is not on the practice of necromancy but on the downfall of Saul.[16] Yet there is no doubt that her ritual is successful. The

11. Pigott, "Wives, Witches, and Wise Women," 154.

12. Pigott, "Wives, Witches, and Wise Women," 154–55.

13. Lust, "On Wizards and Prophets," 133. Another suggestion has been that the woman is actually "throwing" her voice, so that it sounds like it is coming from another location. This is what Saul actually hears, rather than a ghostly voice. Early ideas of this role can be seen in the LXX's use of the word in Greek that means "ventriloquist."

14. Hamori, "The Prophet and the Necromancer," 830.

15. Hamori, "The Prophet and the Necromancer," 843.

16. Hamori, Women's Divination, 119.

ambiguity of the text seems to confuse whether the woman's crying out (v. 12) is due to Samuel's appearance or to the specific request to conjure the prophet most closely associated with King Saul. When she sees Samuel (or his ghost), the medium is startled, not because she knew she was a fake and had not expected anything to appear, but more likely because the stranger's request to contact Samuel reveals to her that he is the king—the very one who has outlawed her profession. "The text makes the point that the woman is afraid of the king, not of the ghost. She was frightened when three anonymous men came to her; now she recognizes one of these men to be her chief enemy."[17] To support this reading, Hamori points out that it is not until the next verse (v. 13) that the medium describes what she sees, so her cry in v. 12 precedes Samuel's appearance.[18]

This scene within the broader story leaves some intriguing images in the minds of the audience. Who besides Saul is present for the experience? Where are his servants during the appearance of Samuel? If only Saul and the woman are in the room when Samuel is brought up, and if Saul cannot see Samuel, then at whose feet does he kneel (v. 14)?

Given the lack of any other visual presence, Saul prostrates himself before the medium "to honour an invisible ancestor."[19] Is this a sign of his accepting her authority over him? The sight of a king (even a disgraced one) kneeling before a woman, who is also a necromancer, is quite unexpected. Clearly, Saul is a weakened king on the verge of being overthrown. Compared to him, the medium is portrayed as strong and authoritative. "The author of the Samuel text presents the necromancer as successful, as the one who finally provides access to divine knowledge, and shows her overall in a remarkably positive light."[20]

A Compassionate Host or a Presider over a Sacrificial Meal?
—2 Samuel 28:20–25

> 20 Immediately Saul fell full length on the ground, filled with fear because of the words of Samuel; and there was no strength in him, for he had eaten nothing all day and all night. 21 The woman came to Saul, and when she saw that he was terrified, she said to him,

17. Reis, "Eating the Blood," 10.

18. Hamori, *Women's Divination*, 121.

19. Fischer, "1 Samuel 28," 33.

20. Hamori, *Women's Divination*, 129.

"Your servant has listened to you; I have taken my life in my hand, and have listened to what you have said to me. 22 Now therefore, you also listen to your servant; let me set a morsel of bread before you. Eat, that you may have strength when you go on your way." 23 He refused, and said, "I will not eat." But his servants, together with the woman, urged him; and he listened to their words. So he got up from the ground and sat on the bed. 24 Now the woman had a fatted calf in the house. She quickly slaughtered it, and she took flour, kneaded it, and baked unleavened cakes. 25 She put them before Saul and his servants, and they ate. Then they rose and went away that night.

In this concluding scene, the woman takes up another role, but the nature of that role is debated. When the communication with Samuel is over, Saul is left lying prostrate on the ground, seemingly exhausted from the whole experience. It is at this point that the woman offers him a meal. Her motivation and the function of that meal are open to much debate as well. First, though, the medium must convince Saul to eat. Her words to the distraught king are not just a mere invitation to eat. She confronts Saul with a proposition based on an equation: I listened to you; now you listen to me. These are not the words that we expect to come from female of low status in addressing a royal. Her words are "expressed with intelligence, delicacy, and tact."[21] There is a sense of authority in her words, and eventually Saul does as she instructs. He gets-up and eats, then he goes away. If, as Uriel Simon suggests, a key theme of the story is "listening to a voice of authority,"[22] Saul's heeding of the medium's words provides the "climax."

For some, the meal prepared by the woman is simply an example of ancient Near Eastern hospitality. There is a guest under her roof, and the societal codes require that she offer him food and drink to go along with the shelter she has already provided. In a manner much like Abraham at the Oaks of Mamre (Gen 18:1–8), she prepares a fatted calf and unleavened bread to feed Saul and his servants. Her generosity is to be admired, especially given that Saul could have her killed now that he has gotten what he came for. In fact, some suggest that the meal was motivated by fear for her own life and her desire to get the king out of her home.[23] Certainly, the story indicates her concern for Saul, who had been fasting, and she knows that he will need physical sustenance to face what lies ahead of him. In a

21. Reis, "Eating the Blood," 13.
22. Hamori, "The Prophet and the Necromancer," 835.
23. Reis, "Eating the Blood," 14.

way, she restores him to life and even provides him "a modicum of his royal dignity," when she twice refers to herself as his "servant" (vv. 21–22).[24]

Other scholars have seen more than hospitality in this act of serving a meal to Saul and his companions. Some have suggested that the medium prepares a "sacred" meal as a conclusion to the séance experience. Of particular interest is the verb used in v. 24, za'bach, which is translated as "sacrifice" or "slaughter for a sacrifice." This is the only place in the Hebrew Bible where the verb occurs in the third-person singular feminine form. This makes the medium "the only woman in the Hebrew Bible who sacrifices alone."[25] Pamela Tamarkin Reis suggests that this meal is an act of sacrifice "to the spirits of the dead in order that Saul will not die as Samuel foretold."[26] Reis also points out that there is no mention of the woman preparing the meat or roasting it, thus leading her to conclude that the meat was "eaten raw with the blood" in it.[27] The sacrifice of the calf has also been suggested as an offering for conjuring up the dead, either as an enticement or in gratitude.[28] Another suggestion is that the meal is honoring Samuel and could have been part of worship within an ancestor cult.[29] Certainly the woman's act of sacrificing the calf aligns with the broader portrayal of her as a ritual expert, but the exact intent of the meal remains a mystery within the biblical text. As Hamori concludes, "The meal may have had a vague connection to the act of divination in the sense that it was a break-fast, but on the not-every-excavated-cup-is-a-ritual-goblet principle, sometimes a meal is just a meal."[30]

There is another interpretation of the woman's feeding of Saul that fits into the overall focus of this book. Many scholars have portrayed the medium as functioning in a motherly role of showing compassion and feeding the "child." In his comparison of Hannah and the medium, Matthew Michael concludes by "motherizing" the medium, who is never described as a mother in the text: "Like a mother taking care of her baby in the representation of Hannah and Samuel, Saul is also represented as being cared

---

24. Simon, "A Balanced Story," 164.
25. Siegel, "The Necromancer's Inheritance," 13.
26. Reis, "Eating the Blood," 14.
27. Reis, "Eating the Blood," 17.
28. Beuken, "The Prophet" 11.
29. Fischer, "1 Samuel 28," 40.
30. Hamori, Women's Divination, 124.

for by a witch."[31] He suggests that we should read the story of the medium at Endor through the lens of "the motherhood of Hannah." While Michael's attention to the fact that these two women appear as a set of bookends to Saul's story is a fruitful insight into the role of gender in 1 Samuel, this does not necessitate imposing motherhood on the necromancer. Rather, this seems to reflect a contemporary reader's need to essentialize all women into an acceptable role of reproduction. Other scholars have also attempted to domesticate the medium into a more comfortable role as a mother, but this denies her position as a ritual expert and initiating agent of the actions that take place in this story.

The Medium of Endor—A Childfree Woman

"The dominant theological voice of the text may be uncomfortable with the image of a famous land-owning woman who possesses the power to summon and offer a communion sacrifice to the spirits of the dead, seeking to deny that power in the same way she has been denied a name."[32] Likewise, modern interpreters who find their piety offended by what is essentially a positive portrayal of this nonconforming woman, who is never condemned in the text, need to recognize her professionalism, courage, wit, power, and compassion. None of these characteristics requires her to be a mother, and it might be that her childfree status allowed her to fulfill her vocation.

Introducing the Wise Woman of Tekoa

In 2 Samuel 14, we are placed amid of the brokenness in King David's family and its tragic consequences. The preceding chapter tells a horrifying story involving rape and murder. One of David's sons, Amnon, rapes his half sister Tamar. Even though David knows about his son's sinful act, he does not seek justice for his daughter. Instead, Tamar's brother Absalom, another of David's many sons, must avenge his sister's rape by having Amnon killed. David is furious and wants revenge for Amnon's murder. Fearing for his life, Absalom flees from Israel in order to avoid conviction and probably execution. After three years have passed, David's grief over Amnon's death has subsided, as has his anger, and he misses Absalom. However, David

---

31. Michael, "Narrative Conjuring or the Tales of Two Sisters?," 486–87.

32. Siegel, "The Necromancer's Inheritance," 15.

realizes that, as king, he will be required to see that on Absalom's return he is punished. David's pride will not allow him to confess to his own wrongdoing in failing to protect his daughter Tamar and to accept at least some responsibility for the murder of Amnon that had taken place. David's military commander, Joab, realizes the king's dilemma, and so he seeks out someone to help bring an end to this family feud.

Although she has no name, the wise woman of Tekoa has a voice and agency within the Davidic Succession Narrative. In fact, she speaks more words than one might expect. She is one of the sixteen individuals who speak more than three times in this section of the Deuteronomistic History. All of the others are identified by name, but she is known only as the wise woman of Tekoa.[33] Her words accomplish several things within the storyline of David's broken family. They create the opportunity for the king to recognize his own shortfall in keeping Absalom in exile. She also confronts the king with his lack of good leadership in this tumultuous time and implies a judgment of David's abandoning Tamar. Ultimately her words convince the king to allow Absalom to return. With authoritative grace, she manipulates David to do the right thing. Although she pretends to be a grieving mother before the king, there is no indication of her connection to motherhood or of her being barren. She is professional female who plays a key role in one of the Hebrew Bible's most important descriptions of the Davidic Royal House.

A Known Professional Woman—2 Samuel 14:1–3

> 1 Now Joab son of Zeruiah perceived that the king's mind was on Absalom. 2 Joab sent to Tekoa and brought from there a wise woman. He said to her, "Pretend to be a mourner; put on mourning garments, do not anoint yourself with oil, but behave like a woman who has been mourning many days for the dead. 3 Go to the king and speak to him as follows." And Joab put the words into her mouth.

It would appear from the text that the renown of the wise woman of Tekoa was widespread in Israel; Joab knows exactly whom to employ for his purposes. He seeks her skills to address the dilemma of his depressed king. However, readers are left guessing by her title (Hebrew, 'eshet hokmah) and lack of a description of her position. While there is no clear proof that

33. Zahavi-Ely, "'Turn Right or Left,'" 46–47.

the wise woman was an official position in cities (though perhaps small towns), there seems to be evidence to support the existence of this important role in the ancient Near East and in the Hebrew Bible. In looking at the broader context of the cultures that surrounded ancient Israel, Esther Hamori points to the wise women mentioned in Hittite literature. She argues that there is a clear indication that "these women held a recognized role in society—that is, these are not references to women who happened to be described as 'wise' (as the titles in 2 Samuel are usually taken), but to a group of people who served a particular function, who were called by a consistent title."[34] Claudia Camp makes a similar claim about the "wise women" in 2 Samuel, arguing that this was one of the possible political roles that women could hold in the premonarchic period of Israel up until at least the Davidic monarchy.[35] It was "a role that we might classify as a regularized set of functions rather than an official position, a definition that accords well with what we can ascertain of that society's tendency toward the diffusion of political functions throughout the community."[36] The fact that the biblical storyteller refers to her only by this adjective and a town also indicates that the audience likely has an understanding and image of a wise woman's role in a community.

The Hebrew word *hakam* is usually translated "wise," and its noun form, *hokmah*, as "wisdom." Within the Hebrew Bible, wisdom is not understood as simply being smart or knowing a set of data. Rather, its range of meanings includes skill or ability, cunning or cleverness, and even a sailor's skill of steering a ship. Wisdom carries the sense of what guides one through the sea of life, an understanding of the rules of the game of life. For a person to be described as wise, they would have to demonstrate such wisdom as well as other characteristics. Leah Kohn points out that "torah wisdom also involves maintaining a balance between the opposite extremes embedded in one's personality . . . Wisdom is then the ability to assess which and how much of one side should be put forward—and at what optimal time."[37] Brenner-Idan writes that "these [wise] women are clever, articulate, involved in the political life of the community—in short, they enjoy a status similar to that of an elder, or a 'wise man.'"[38] In the case

---

34. Hamori, *Women's Divination*, 134.

35. Camp, "The Wise Women of 2 Samuel," 14.

36. Camp, "The Wise Women of 2 Samuel," 15.

37. Kohn, "The Woman of Tekoa."

38. Brenner-Idan, *The Israelite Woman*, 38.

of the wise woman of Tekoa, her wisdom is displayed in her cunning ability to speak the words that need to be heard in the particular case of David and Absalom, navigating the difficult waters of political power and familial relationships.

The role of the wise woman carries a clear sense of authority; her words are to be heard and heeded. The fact that Joab has selected the wise woman of Tekoa to accuse the king of wrongdoing indicates her influence. She can say to the king what Joab is not able (or willing) to say. Her reception within the story also attests to her recognized authority. Certainly some question both her authority and her wisdom, based on 2 Sam 14:3b. The text states that Joab puts "the words into her mouth," but what exactly he tells her is unclear. The wise woman has a specialized role, and the military commander has gone to some trouble to seek her out and present her to the king. "She is clearly not just any woman pulled in to deliver Joab's lines; surely someone in all of Jerusalem could have done well enough at that."[39] Even if he told her exactly what to say, this does not necessarily detract from her importance and authority. The phrase "put the words in (someone's) mouth" is found in other places within the Hebrew Bible, where the recipients of such "words" are also persons with authority. One example is Exod 4:10–16, where Moses puts words in the mouth of Aaron. Within this story, it is clear that "the authority which inheres in the words put in someone's mouth can be considered separately from the personal authority that that individual carries."[40] The wise woman's authority comes from the way she delivers those words and from her timing. Her cunning and quick wit are the tools she employs to confront and condemn the king. There is yet another way to interpret this phrase "Joab put the words in her mouth." The Hebrew word *de'barim*, translated as "words" in v. 3, can also mean "things" or even "ideas." Probably what Joab tells the wise woman is information about the situation between Absalom and David, things she needs to know in order to choose the appropriate story to tell in order to help bring about reconciliation between a father and his son.

A Prophetic Storyteller—2 Samuel 14:4–11

4 When the woman of Tekoa came to the king, she fell on her face to the ground and did obeisance, and said, "Help, O king!" 5 The

39. Hamori, *Women's Divination*, 139.
40. Camp, "The Wise Women in 2 Samuel," 18.

king asked her, "What is your trouble?" She answered, "Alas, I am a widow; my husband is dead. 6 Your servant had two sons, and they fought with one another in the field; there was no one to part them, and one struck the other and killed him. 7 Now the whole family has risen against your servant. They say, "Give up the man who struck his brother, so that we may kill him for the life of his brother whom he murdered, even if we destroy the heir as well.' Thus they would quench my one remaining ember, and leave to my husband neither name nor remnant on the face of the earth." 8 Then the king said to the woman, "Go to your house, and I will give orders concerning you." 9 The woman of Tekoa said to the king, "On me be the guilt, my lord the king, and on my father's house; let the king and his throne be guiltless." 10 The king said, "If anyone says anything to you, bring him to me, and he shall never touch you again." 11 Then she said, "Please, may the king keep the Lord your God in mind, so that the avenger of blood may kill no more, and my son not be destroyed." He said, "As the Lord lives, not one hair of your son shall fall to the ground."

In the next scene, the wise woman is granted an audience with the king. Transformed into a mourning widow, she tells the unsuspecting David a story, which is actually an ancient parable of sibling rivalry and resulting fratricide (Gen 4). She relates how her two sons were fighting and one of them killed the other. Now, the rest of her family demands that her one remaining son be put to death for murdering his brother. She is distraught at the thought of losing both of her children and the end of her family's future. Her passionate words draw the king into the narrative, and moved with compassion by her convincing story, David assures the woman that he will grant clemency to her son, and that she can return to her house in peace.

It is important to note that the wise woman is pretending to be a mother and a widow. This does not indicate that she is actually a biological mother. It is a role that she is playing, and it is reliant upon the particular parable she tells and the context of her audience. For the story to parallel David's family situation, there must be two brothers. As the one granted an audience with the king, she most naturally presents as the distraught mother because that role will seem probable and less threatening to the king. Yet some scholars have used the wise woman's parable to argue that her role as a wise woman is directly connected to motherhood. One scholar concludes that the "real issue . . . centers around the life of children or the desire for their survival."[41] While the parable and its direct application do relate to the survival of offspring, there is no reason to assume that the wise woman is a mother, or that her authority comes from having birthed children. As her prophetic words demonstrate in the next section, she has a deeper message to deliver, which goes beyond familial concerns and extends to the whole community.

Based on these verses, it seems one role that wise women might have fulfilled in Israel was that of the community's storyteller. Perhaps her wisdom came from her familiarity with the ancient stories and her ability to know which story to tell at just the right time. In his work, "Women Storytellers in Ancient Israel," Anthony F. Campbell makes a similar connection. He states that "palace singers were among the storytellers of Israel . . . we have evidence for the existence of Israel's storytellers and for their being both men and women."[42] The talent of the wise woman of Tekoa rests not only in choosing the appropriate story but also in "her ability to articulate the parable for the king, within what must have been the intimidating setting of his royal court."[43] Even when the king tries to give a cautious response (2 Sam 14:8), she does not let him off the hook, persisting until David declares that the surviving son will be protected from vengeance. She has aptly used a bit of "juridical trickery" to "create two conditions—of distancing and reinvolvement—necessary for a person blinded by proximity to a problem to achieve a new perspective."[44] Now she can use the king's judgment against himself.

A Confrontational Prophet—2 Samuel 14:12–17

12 Then the woman said, "Please let your servant speak a word to my lord the king." He said, "Speak." 13 The woman said, "Why then have you planned such a thing against the people of God? For in giving this decision the king convicts himself, inasmuch as the king does not bring his banished one home again. 14 We must all die; we are like water spilled on the ground, which cannot be gathered up. But God will not take away a life; God will devise plans so as not to keep an outcast banished forever from his presence. 15 Now I have come to say this to my lord the king because the

41. Olojede, "Women and the Cry for Justice," 764.

42. Campbell, "Women Storytellers," 73.

43. Kohn, "The Woman of Tekoa."

44. Camp, "The Wise Women of 2 Samuel," 21.

people have made me afraid; your servant thought, "I will speak
to the king; it may be that the king will perform the request of his
servant. 16 For the king will hear, and deliver his servant from the
hand of the man who would cut both me and my son off from the
heritage of God.' 17 Your servant thought, "The word of my lord
the king will set me at rest'; for my lord the king is like the angel of
God, discerning good and evil. The Lord your God be with you!"

Although the king believes he has settled the case and can move on to other
things on his agenda, the wise woman is not finished. After being granted
more time in the king's presence, she springs the trap, declaring that David
is as guilty as the avenging family members in the parable. At this point,
another role of a wise woman emerges; she is also a prophet, telling the
king what he needs to hear, even if it's not what he wants to hear. Echoing
the prophet Nathan's words, "'You are the man!'" (2 Sam 12:7), this prophet
proclaims judgment against David for keeping Absalom banished. Her role
as a prophet, and as a wise woman, is also enhanced by the fact that she
comes from Tekoa, the location of another great prophet, Amos (see Amos
1:1).

While some may object to this label of prophet for this wise woman, it
does not seem to be a stretch. There are examples in the Hebrew Bible (and
in the ancient Near East) of wise men fulfilling divinatory roles, so why
would the same not hold true for wise women? There is evidence among
Hittite literature that in their culture so-called wise women were also seen
as diviners. In support of the title of prophet for the wise woman of Tekoa,
Hamori writes that "from the wise woman's mouth we see a view of (*hok-mah*) as privileged divine knowledge."[45] Like Nathan before her, and like
the many prophets who follow in the biblical story, she is able to tell the
king that he is in the wrong not just for keeping Absalom in exile but also
for failing to seek justice for Tamar, his daughter. A closer look at the wise
woman's parable reveals that it is not merely a story of two brothers fighting
to the death, but it is about how no one intervened to stop the violence.
Likewise, David does not intervene on behalf of Tamar in order to bring
Amnon to justice, which also could have prevented Absalom's seeking revenge for his sister. For two years, it was within David's hands as the king to

45. Hamori, *Women's Divination*, 140. Hamori later makes the point that at the time
of her writing, there was no published recognition of this prophetic element in the role
of a wise woman (147).

stop the killing before it had begun. Yet, he does nothing. Once again, this wise woman and prophet has convicted the king for his inaction.[46]

While the focus in this story is on the specific brokenness between David and his son, the wise woman of Tekoa takes her opportunity to address a broader concern for justice and mercy in the human family and to connect to God's story the ancient parable she tells. Her prophecy takes the intrafamilial conflict to the wider focus of how it effects the broader community. She seems to draw again from community lore, offering a proverb as part of her chastisement of the king. Her use of the proverb in v. 14 adds wisdom and depth to her earlier parable and to the king's inaction on behalf of his son (and also on behalf of his daughter Tamar). Claudia Camp describes her use of the proverb in v. 14 as "a shining example of a proverb 'in action,' perhaps a reference to a well-known saying rather than a full citation. It is a proverb not nestled quietly in a collection but employed by a person of agile mind and persuasive tongue to influence a situation."[47] In pointing out David's sin, she also makes important claims about community and about God. She declares that what the king has done has implications for the rest of the people in Israel: "Why then have you planned such a thing against the people of God?" (v. 13). The turmoil in his own family prevents the king from assuring the safety and well-being of those under his rule. When there is brokenness anywhere within the human family, no one can know wholeness. The wise woman also offers an alternative view to that of the human desire for vengeance and violence, which creates alienation among God's children and strains humanity's relationship with God. "Regardless of how one interprets her motives and the effectiveness of her argumentation, the wise woman of Tekoa functions as a catalyst for change in the kingship of Israel."[48] She creates an opportunity for reconciliation in the king's broken relationship. After their meeting, David sends word to Absalom that it is safe to come home.

---

46. Hamori, *Women's Divination*, 140. This reading of the parable might address a pressing question for contemporary readers: Why didn't the wise woman speak out on behalf of Tamar? It is not a satisfactory answer, but it is a possible one.

47. Camp, "The Wise Women of 2 Samuel," 20.

48. Pigott, "Wives, Witches, and Wise Women," 160.

A Wise Diplomat—2 Samuel 14:18–20

> 18 Then the king answered the woman, "Do not withhold from me anything I ask you." The woman said, "Let my lord the king speak." 19 The king said, "Is the hand of Joab with you in all this?" The woman answered and said, "As surely as you live, my lord the king, one cannot turn right or left from anything that my lord the king has said. For it was your servant Joab who commanded me; it was he who put all these words into the mouth of your servant. 20 In order to change the course of affairs your servant Joab did this. But my lord has wisdom like the wisdom of the angel of God to know all things that are on the earth."

At this point, David realizes he has been the victim of some covert plan. The woman whom he thought was a distraught widow has gone out of character and confronted him on the throne. Was this all a ruse to get Absalom home? If so, who was behind the plot? The tables are turned, and the king asks a question of the wise woman. He wants to know if Joab is behind this trickery. To her credit, the wise woman does not try to lie before the king. Couching her response in thick flattery, she confesses that it is Joab who sent her. She even lays the blame for the whole encounter at Joab's feet by claiming that he had "put all those words [or ideas] into the mouth of your servant" (1 Sam 14:19). She does, however, try to put in a positive word for Joab by telling the king that his military commander's intentions were good—to ease David's suffering—even if the method was not straightforward. Just as smoothly as the wise woman had transitioned from a grieving mother to a prophet, she now transitions once more into a shrewd diplomat. Clearly, this is a dangerous situation in which she finds herself. It is very possible that David will be angry at being manipulated and will direct that anger at the messenger. "Thus it is not surprising to find the woman lauding the king's superlative wisdom, and couching her admission of trickery as fulsome praise."[49] Part of her role as a wise woman is to be a diplomat, to know the right thing to say at the right moment. "It is improbable that any but a person practiced in the art of confrontation (and manipulation?) could have managed this situation effectively."[50]

---

49. Zahavi-Ely, "'Turn Right or Left,'" 45.

50. Camp, "The Wise Women in 2 Samuel," 18n8.

The Wise Woman of Tekoa—A Childfree Woman

In each aspect of this scene between the wise woman of Tekoa and men of power, she demonstrates not only wisdom but also effective storytelling, prophetic courage, and shrewd diplomacy. She speaks boldly to the most powerful man in the kingdom, and she does so with cunning and grace under fire. In fact, she has one of the longest recorded conversations that David is described as having with a woman. She does all of this based solely on her title, wise woman, without any connection to a man or a list of children she produced. Even with this blatant portrayal of her as anything but a mother, many scholars have tried to fit her into this more expected role. They argue that any authority a wise woman has must be developed from her role as mother. One writes that "wives and mothers known for their common-sense teachings and ability to resolve conflicts might be drafted into the service of their neighborhoods, towns or cities. Such women are found in 2 Samuel as 'wise women.'"[51] Another scholar states that this authority of the wise woman is directly connected to raising children, concluding that "whatever her subsequent training, the wise woman probably gained her first experience in the use of such language (and the recognition of her peers) in the training of her immediate family."[52] But, if there is no reference to motherhood in regard to this wise woman, must the conclusion be that she first had to be a mother and then maybe a grandmother in order to eventually reach this position? If the title is somehow connected to age, then it is highly unlikely that a woman who endured the perils of pregnancy and birth would have survived even to the average life expectancy of thirty.[53] Rather, it is much more likely that this wise woman and her sisters in the guild were trained professionals, skilled in the nuances and lore of their people's wisdom, who attained the status of elders because they were childfree.

---

51. Fontaine, *Smooth Words*, 65. Hamori states that Fontaine's conclusion about wise women is that they are "essential local den mothers" (Hamori, *Women's Divination*, 144n38).

52. Camp, "The Wise Women of 2 Samuel," 25.

53. Some interpreters have suggested that Sarah reached such the advanced age of 127 because she had not birthed any children.

Introducing the Wise Woman of Abel

A second time in 2 Samuel we are introduced to a wise woman. Although her story is fairly brief, it contributes more to our understanding of this female role. The work of the wise woman of Tekoa opens the door for Absalom's return, but things do not go well. A rebellion begins against David, and we join the story with Joab on the chase for one of the rebels, Sheba. When Sheba takes refuge in the town of Abel (of Beth-maacah), Joab and his forces attack the city with the apparent intention of catching the fugitive no matter what the collateral damage may be. With the town at the mercy of Joab's forces, the townspeople desperately need a hero to save them from certain doom. While biblical readers might expect a male to step forward, that is not what happens. Instead, it will be a wise woman who dares to address the military commander and negotiate a truce between Joab and Abel. Once again, the title of wise woman is all we are given for this hero without a name. She too is not presented as connected to any male (husband, brother, or father), and there is no mention of any children. Despite the woman's childfree status in this story, many interpreters once again have tried to make her a mother. In fact, some have suggested that her phrase "mother in Israel" to describe the town of Abel (2 Sam 20:19) should be understood as a description of herself.[54] Could it be that these interpreters read into the text their own biases that require a female character to be a mother, even a symbolic one? This wise woman has authority and negotiating skills that do not involve her womb, and perhaps she is in this position because she is childfree.

A Defender of the City—2 Samuel 20:15–21

15 Joab's forces came and besieged [Sheba] in Abel of Beth-maacah; they threw up a siege ramp against the city, and it stood against the rampart. Joab's forces were battering the wall to break it down. 16 Then a wise woman called from the city, "Listen! Listen! Tell Joab, "Come here, I want to speak to you." 17 He came near her; and the woman said, "Are you Joab?" He answered, "I am." Then she said to him, "Listen to the words of your servant." He answered, "I am listening." 18 Then she said, "They used to say in the old days, 'Let them inquire at Abel'; and so they would settle a matter. 19 I

54. See Lockyer, *All the Women of the Bible*; and Camp, "Wise Woman of Abel Beth-Maacah: Bible."

am one of those who are peaceable and faithful in Israel; you seek to destroy a city that is a mother in Israel; why will you swallow up the heritage of the Lord?" 20 Joab answered, "Far be it from me, far be it, that I should swallow up or destroy! 21 That is not the case! But a man of the hill country of Ephraim, called Sheba son of Bichri, has lifted up his hand against King David; give him up alone, and I will withdraw from the city." The woman said to Joab, "His head shall be thrown over the wall to you."

The siege of Abel of Beth-maacah, begun by Joab, has the potential to destroy the city and all of its inhabitants. Sheba's presence there endangers the whole community. At this important juncture, as the city teeters on the edge of destruction, one among them takes up the challenge of confronting Joab and learning the reason for the attack. This wise woman must have some authority within the city in that she can negotiate a desirable outcome for the community. In addition, Joab seems to have a certain level of respect for the unnamed woman, as he responds to her summons, answers her question, and listens to her words. From this encounter between Joab and the wise woman, we can glean more information about how the role of wise woman was understood in the ancient storytellers' imaginations, and perhaps in their culture.

Once the woman gets Joab's attention and agreement to listen to her "words" (v. 17), she begins with a brief bit of the city's history. She states that Abel of Beth-macaah was once a place for people to seek answers to disputes or questions: "They used to say in the old days, 'Let them inquire at Abel'; and so they would settle a matter" (2 Sam 20:18). Some have identified this description of the town of Abel as a proverb, but its "precise content is somewhat uncertain because of textual difficulties."[55] If this ancient description of Abel is correct, then its utterance by this nameless woman links her as a speaker in 2 Sam 20:18–19 to the wise woman of Tekoa, who also recites a vague proverb. Another possible interpretation of the saying is that it refers to the importance of Abel in the history of Israel. In other ancient cultures, there were towns where people would go to seek answers or insight from an oracle, and perhaps Abel has a similar reputation and tradition. There are possible archeological findings to support this idea. In 2018, archeologists digging in the location of Abel of Beth-macaah uncovered a shrine that they suggested was the location where people would

---

55. Camp, "The Wise Women of 2 Samuel," 19.

have sought an oracle to provide answers and insight.[56] Even without this possible evidence, the wise woman is educating Joab about the city's reputation.[57] She identifies herself as among those "who are peaceable and faithful in Israel" (v. 19a) indicating that there is no reason for Joab to attack Abel. Whether she is quoting a parable or referring to the role of the city, the wise woman is "utilizing the art of wisdom speech to an end often associated with ancient Near Eastern wisdom literature, viz., the persuasion of a ruler by a soft tongue in a delicate situation (cf. Prov 25:15; 15:1)."[58]

Her next words, though, are accusatory. She demands to know why Joab would want to destroy a peaceful and renowned city. The woman describes Abel in two more ways: as "a mother in Israel" (v. 19b) and as "the heritage of the Lord" (v. 19c). Both descriptions of the city are clearly metaphors, not to be taken literally, but their meanings are not so clear. How can a city be a "mother"?[59] This particular phrase in v. 19b is found in only one other place in the Hebrew Bible—Judg 5:7—where it is used to describe Deborah, who is not presented as a biological mother. Considering this usage of the phrase, it is clear that a "mother in Israel" cannot indicate a woman who has given birth to children; a city cannot produce offspring. It is a metaphor that provides insight into the city's reputation and a justification for why Joab should not attack Abel. Perhaps it indicates protection, counsel, or both. The other description of the city, "the heritage of the Lord" is placed in parallel relationship with "mother in Israel." Its meaning is also unclear. Hamori suggests it "may refer either to Abel as the seat of oracular inquiry or to the woman's role in it (or perhaps both)."[60] The implication of both phrases does seem clear. The wise woman is shaming Joab for daring to attack and destroy an important city and its peaceful inhabitants. The accusation gets the desired response. Joab immediately clarifies that his beef is not with the people of Abel but with the rebellious Sheba. He is all that

56. Bohstrom, "Archaeologists Find Signs of 3,000-Year-Old Oracle Cult."

57. Hamori, *Women's Divination*, 146.

58. Camp, "The Wise Women of 2 Samuel," 19.

59. Hamori (*Women's Divination*, 142) argues that "a mother in Israel" should be understood as referring to the wise woman herself and not the city. Ackerman (*Warrior*, 42) agrees that this is the simplest explanation, especially given the phrase's use in Judg 5 to describe Deborah. She links these two women by saying that both women provide desired counsel for their people (Ackerman, *Warrior*, 62). Hamori, however (*Women's Divination*, 143), adds that both Deborah and the wise woman of Abel are involved with divination.

60. Hamori, *Women's Divination*, 142.

Joab and his soldiers want. Her quick response attests to the authority of the wise woman. She assures Joab that Sheba will meet the end the king requires, and she will provide evidence of his demise (v. 21). The wise woman uses "psychological pressure to attain her goal of halting Joab's siege."[61]

An Adviser for the City—2 Samuel 20:22

22 Then the woman went to all the people with her wise plan. And they cut off the head of Sheba son of Bichri, and threw it out to Joab. So he blew the trumpet, and they dispersed from the city, and all went to their homes, while Joab returned to Jerusalem to the king.

Now, it is time for the wise woman to make good on her promise of Sheba's head to Joab. She stands before the people of Abel, or at least a decision-making body, and presents the facts of the situation, along with her proposal. It is interesting to note that her plan is described as "wise" in v. 22a. Would you expect any less from a wise woman? To save the city, they must behead Sheba and throw his head over the wall. This will put an end to the military siege. Here again, it appears that she has unquestioned authority. Like a court advisor, she counsels the people about the appropriate action to take, and they heed her advice.[62] Sheba's head is thrown over the wall, and Joab takes his troops away from Abel.

The Wise Woman of Abel—A Childfree Woman

The words of the wise woman of Abel carry great weight in the hearing of both the military commander, Joab, and the people of the city. It seems everyone responds to her call. Having saved her people, the wise woman can go to her home the hero of the day. She is remembered not as a mother or as barren but as a wise counselor and brave leader who protects her hometown. "Sagacity, faithfulness, a commanding presence, and readily acknowledged influence with her peers—these are the attributes that clearly mark this woman."[63]

61. Camp, "The Wise Women of 2 Samuel," 22.

62. Camp, "The Wise Women of 2 Samuel," 18.

63. Camp, "The Wise Women of 2 Samuel," 26.

Conclusions—Three Childfree Women

These three unnamed women play key roles at important junctures in Israel's story. Without obligations to husbands or children, they are able to fill professional positions that include ritual expert, diviner, prophet, political advisor, and more. Their presence in the biblical text "reveals *par example* the broad spectrum of divine consultation, solicited and unsolicited, which was apparently dependent on a broad range of religious practitioners such as seers, augurs, ecstatics, men of god, wise women, godmothers and so on."[64] Whether sought out for their professional services or stepping forward at just the right moment, the women demonstrate concern for their community on both an individual and national level. In his work *Weisheit und Tat der Frauen*, Martin Buber identifies two shared characteristics of these women: "they act decisively in the face of adversity, and they stand for faithfulness and reconciliation."[65] The medium and the wise women are involved in communication, on a divine and human level. They are free to pursue their vocations even in situations where their work is dangerous or even outlawed. While few and far between within the Hebrew Bible, these women demonstrate that the biblical storytellers have no trouble portraying female characters in important roles without regard to their wombs. The nonchalance with which they appear in the biblical stories also teaches us that the ancient audience had no problem hearing words of warning and advice from the mouths of women.[66] "Hence 'wise woman,' like 'medium,' would appear to denote a profession or prominent social role rather than a one-time activity or character trait."[67] These women use their skills, wisdom, and cunning to move the story of Israel into the future. They do all of this without producing offspring.

We are a Medium and Two Sages . . .

I am the Medium of Endor . . .

I was once a respected ritual expert, . . . but now you call me a witch.

---

64. Dijkstra, "Prophets, Men of God, Wise Women," 12.
65. Schwartz, "The Wisdom of Women," referencing Martin Buber, 11.
66. Goitein and Carasik, "Women as Creators of Biblical Genres," 9.
67. Reinhartz, "Anonymity and Character," 134.

I am the Wise Woman of Tekoa . . .

I was a prophetic sage and advisor to the king, . . . but nobody remembers my name.

I am the Wise Woman of Abel . . .

I negotiated a ceasefire and saved my people, . . . but no one knows my name.

8

CHILDFREE WOMEN

Ancient and Modern

Our study of childfree women has identified female characters who, working with the Divine, play amazing roles in the stories of the Hebrew Bible. While there is no decisive evidence that women actually filled such leadership positions in the cultures behind these narratives, there exists both the possibility and the probability that storytellers reflected their lived experience. From extrabiblical evidence, it seems probable that Israel also incorporated females into similar positions of power and influence. The male-dominated focus of the final product (the Hebrew Bible) may have minimized the roles women played or even erased their influence, and names, from the sacred texts. Yet if this was the intent, these female characters defy being dismissed and having their lives reduced to their reproductive potential or lack thereof. When we read with a feminist, childfree, liberative hermeneutic, we can identify the actions of these women as similar to if not the same as roles supposedly reserved for men. Without assuming motherhood for every female character, we discover women who are indeed more than a womb.

Based on this examination of the texts about childfree women, there does seem to be a difference in the Hebrew Bible between being barren and being childfree. I am not the first person to recognize this distinction or the first to identify women in the biblical texts who never are described as mothers but who have played important roles in the story of Israel. However, the focus on this particular shared trait of these women and my quest to see the value of their contributions to the biblical story on their own merits, without some connection to motherhood, does seem to be unique. By focusing on what the texts reveal about these female characters, and not trying to read behind the texts (i.e., whether these women "really" had children), I can conclude that there exists within the Hebrew Bible the possibility that a woman's not having offspring was seen not as a restriction or a curse but instead as a viable option and a pathway to broader or different participation in communal life.

Roles of Women Represented in the Hebrew Bible

In reading the stories of the Hebrew Bible, there is no doubt that women played many important roles within a self-sustaining household, but their influence and actions did not stop there. Though few and far between, there are female characters in the Hebrew Bible who are portrayed in roles that do not require motherhood or may have even excluded any reproductive role. In the preceding chapters, we have considered eight female characters who are never described as biological mothers, nor are they described as barren.[1] Among the texts dealing with these women, they are portrayed as fulfilling a wide range of roles in the story of ancient Israel, many of which are predominantly reserved for males. These females are presented as leaders within the realms of government and religion. In government they fill positions of royal advisor, politician, strategist, judge, sage, entrepreneur, negotiator, warrior, scribe, reformer, queen, and liberator. Their religious roles include prophet-diviner, poet, ritual expert, worship leader, textual critic, and canonizer.

Whether the roles identified above were actually filled by Israelite women or not, it is important to note that the biblical storytellers and writers could imagine this being the case. They preserved such stories for audiences that may have been less familiar with such female leaders, or perhaps the audiences were not surprised at all. These stories reminded readers and hearers "that ideologically-construed gender expectations may and have

---

1. In future research, I would like to explore the extracanonical characters of Judith and Susanna. Both of them are portrayed as childfree. In particular, Judith defies any claim for motherhood and fills a role that many would associate with only males. The parallels between Jael and Judith would provide much fodder for expanding our assumptions and stereotypes about what it means to be female.

been transgressed in the past and with good results."[2] There seems to be evidence that at least in the time when texts of the Hebrew Bible were being finalized (perhaps the Persian period), women were not seen as nothing more than "walking womb-bearers for their husbands/mates, with absolutely no significance of their own."[3]

Implications for Today

My research on these women who are not identified as biological mothers or as barren lends support to the conclusion that the Hebrew Bible portrays these women as valuable without a procreative role. These findings could provide an alternative for women who look to the biblical texts as resources for their self-identity so that they may define themselves in ways that are no longer bound by the religious and social assumption that motherhood is essential to womanhood. This is not the same as co-opting whatever women do as some form of mothering. It requires an expansion of our definition of femininity that is not based on fertility. We will need to recognize childbearing as an option, not an obligation, and to see childfree women as spiritually, psychologically, and physically complete, just like their sisters with children.[4] Indeed all females are more than wombs.

One of the unexpected outcomes of my research for this book was the discovery of a growing community of individuals or couples who do not have children by choice. There is a web circle dedicated solely to sites that offer support, and at times justification, for those who choose this path. Two domain names of particular interest are thenotmom.com and livechildfree.com. One of the earliest and most fully developed websites is childfree.net, which describes the intentional move to stop using the adjective *childless*, which indicates loss or incompleteness, and to adopt the term *childfree*, though this term has its own negative connotations. The creators of the website childfree.net give the following reason for why a website on living childfree is even necessary: "Being childfree-by-choice is frowned upon in our kid-centric society . . . We feel like freaks and do not realize exactly how many of us there are."[5] It has been my experience, and I'm sure the experience of others, that religious communities can be some of

2. Labahn and Ben Zvi, "Observations on Women," 457.

3. Labahn and Ben Zvi, "Observations on Women," 465.

4. Cain, *The Childless Revolution*, 147.

5. Childfree.net, "Why a Website?"

the most inhospitable places for childfree persons. Biblical texts are often the ammunition used to denigrate women in particular for not fulfilling the divine mandate that they "be fruitful and multiply." If the stories of childfree women in the Hebrew Bible were told and their actions celebrated and not "motherized," not only could childfree female churchgoers find a place for them in the work of the Holy, but everyone would be challenged to break free of pronatalist stereotypes and to expand our views of gender and sexuality.

BIBLIOGRAPHY

Achtelstetter, Karen. "Huldah at the Table: Reflections on Leadership and the Leadership of Women." *Currents in Theology and Mission* 37 (2010) 176–84.

Ackerman, Susan. "Digging Up Deborah: Recent Hebrew Bible Scholarship on Gender and the Contribution of Archeology." *Near Eastern Archeology* 66 (2003) 172–84.

———. "The Queen Mother and the Cult in Ancient Israel." *Journal of Biblical Literature* 112 (1993) 385–401.

———. *Warrior, Dancer, Seductress, Queen: Women in Judges and Biblical Israel.* Anchor Bible Reference Library. New York: Doubleday, 1998.

Armstrong, Karen. *The Gospel according to Woman: Christianity's Creation of the Sex War in the West.* Garden City, NY: Anchor, 1986.

Beauvoir, Simone de. *The Second Sex.* Translated by H. M. Parshley. New York: Vintage, 1974.

Beckman, Gary. "Birth and Motherhood among the Hittites." In *Women in Antiquity: Real Women across the Ancient World,* edited by Stephanie Lynn Budin and Jean MacIntosh Turfa, 319–28. Rewriting Antiquity. London: Routledge, 2016.

Bergmann, Claudia D. *Childbirth as a Metaphor for Crisis: Evidence from the Ancient Near East, the Hebrew Bible and IQH XI.* Beihefte zur Zeitschrift für die alttestamentliche Wissenschaft 382. Berlin: de Gruyter, 2008.

Berlin, Adele. *Esther: The Traditional Hebrew Text with the New JPS Translation.* The JPS Commentary. Philadelphia: Jewish Publication Society, 2001.

Bertman, Stephen. *Handbook to Life in Ancient Mesopotamia.* Facts on File Library of World History. New York: Facts on File, 2003.

Beuken, W. A. M. "The Prophet as 'Hammer of Witches.'" *Journal for the Study of the Old Testament* 6 (1978) 3–17.

Bird, Phyllis A. *Missing Persons and Mistaken Identities: Women and Gender in Ancient Israel.* Overtures to Biblical Theology. Minneapolis: Fortress, 1997.

———. "What Makes a Feminist Reading Feminist? A Qualified Answer." In *Escaping Eden: New Feminist Perspectives on the Bible,* edited by Harold C. Washington et al., 124–31. New York: New York University Press, 1999

Block, Daniel I. "The Period of the Judges: Religious Disintegration under Tribal Rule." In *Israel's Apostasy and Restoration: Essays in Honor of Roland K. Harrison,* edited by Avraham Gileadi, 39–57. Grand Rapids: Baker, 1988.

Boesak, Allan A. "The Riverbank, the Seashore and the Wilderness: Miriam, Liberation and Prophetic Witness against Empire." *HTS Teologiese Studies/Theological Studies* 73 (2017) 1–15.

Bohstrom, Philippe. "Archaeologists Find Signs of 3,000-Year-Old Oracle Cult in Ancient Israel." *Haaretz*, September 17, 2018. https://www.haaretz.com/israel-news/.premium.MAGAZINE-signs-of-3-000-year-old-oracle-cult-found-in-israel-archaeology-1.6472911/.

Bombeck, Erma. *Motherhood: The Second Oldest Profession.* New York: McGraw-Hill, 1983.

Brenner-Idan, Athalya. *The Israelite Woman: Social Role and Literary Type in Biblical Narrative.* 2nd ed. Cornerstones. London: Bloomsbury, 2015.

Brenner(-Idan), Athalya, and Fokkelien van Dijk-Hemmes. *On Gendering Texts: Female and Male Voices in the Hebrew Bible.* 2nd ed. Biblical Interpretations Series 1. Leiden: Brill, 1996.

Brettler, Marc Zvi. *The Book of Judges.* Old Testament Readings. London: Routledge, 2002.

Bronner, Leila Leah. "Reclaiming Esther: From Sex Object to Sage." *Jewish Bible Quarterly* 26 (1998) 3–11.

———. *Stories of Biblical Mothers: Maternal Power in the Hebrew Bible.* Lanham, MD: University of America Press, 2004.

Brown, John Pairman. "The Mediterranean Seer and Shamanism." *Zeitschrift für die alttestamentliche Wissenschaft* 93 (1981) 374–400.

Budin Stephanie Lynn, and Jean MacIntosh Turfa, eds. *Women in Antiquity: Real Women across the Ancient World.* Rewriting Antiquity. London: Routledge, 2016.

Cain, Madelyn. *The Childless Revolution: What it Means to be Childless Today.* New York: Perseus, 2001.

Camp, Claudia V. "Huldah." In *Women in Scripture: A Dictionary of Named and Unnamed Women in the Hebrew Bible, the Apocryphal/Deuterocanonical Books, and the New Testament,* edited by Carol Meyers, et al, 96–97. Boston: Houghton Mifflin, 2000.

———. "Huldah: Bible." *Jewish Women: A Comprehensive Historical Encyclopedia.* (2009). https://jwa.org/encyclopedia/article/huldah-bible/.

———. "Wise Woman of Abel Beth-Maacah: Bible." *Jewish Women's Archive* (website). *The Encyclopedia of Jewish Women.* https://jwa.org/encyclopedia/article/wise-woman-of-abel-beth-maacah-bible/.

———. "The Wise Women of 2 Samuel: A Role Model for Women in Early Israel?" *Catholic Biblical Quarterly* 43 (1981) 14–29.

Campbell, Antony F. "Women Storytellers in Ancient Israel." *Australian Biblical Review* 48 (2000) 72–73.

Centers for Disease Control and Prevention. Reproductive Health. "Infertility FAQs." (webpage). https://www.cdc.gov/reproductivehealth/infertility/index.htm/.

Childfree.net. "Why a Website?" http://www.childfree.net/.

Cogan, Mordechai, and Hayim Tadmor. *II Kings: A New Translation with Introduction and Commentary.* Anchor Bible 11. Garden City, NY: Doubleday, 1988.

Cohen, Eric. "Why Have Children?" *Commentary* (2006) 44–49.

Cohn, Robin. "Rabbi Huldah." *Robin Cohn: Women of the Bible for Thinkers* (website), August 31, 2010. http://robincohn.net/rabbi-huldah/.

Collins, Billie Jean. "Women in Hittite Religion." In *Women In Antiquity: Real Women across the Ancient World,* edited by Stephanie Lynn Budin and Jean MacIntosh Turfa, 329–40. Rewriting Antiquity. London: Routledge, 2016.

Costas, Orlando E. "The Subversiveness of Faith: Esther as a Paradigm for a Liberating Theology." *Ecumenical Review* 40 (1988) 66–78.

Craigie, Peter C. "Deborah and Anat: A Study of Poetic Imagery (Judges 5)." *Zeitschrift für die alttestamentliche Wissenschaft* 90 (2009) 374–81.

Cross, Frank M., and David N. Freedman. "The Song of Miriam." *Journal of Near Eastern Studies* 14 (1955) 237–50.

Davison, Lisa Wilson. *Preaching the Women of the Bible*. St. Louis: Chalice, 2006.

Deffinbaugh, Bob. "3. Esther's Dilemma and Decision (Esther 4:1–17)." From *Esther: A Study in Divine Providence*. *Bible.org* (website), February 2, 2009, https://bible.org/seriespage/3-esther-s-dilemma-and-decision-esther-41-17/.

Dijkstra, Meindert. "Prophets, Men of God, Wise Women: Dreams and Prophecies in Hittite Stories." In *Prophecy and Prophets in Stories: Papers Read at the Fifth Meeting of the Edinburgh Prophecy Network, Utrecht, October 2013*, edited by Bob Becking and Hans M. Barstad, 11–25. Oudtestamentische Studiën 65. Leiden: Brill, 2015.

Duran, Nicole. "Who Wants to Marry a Persian King? Gender Games and Wars and the Book of Esther." In *Pregnant Passion: Gender, Sex and Violence in the Bible*, edited by Cheryl A. Kirk-Duggan, 71–84. Semeia Studies 44. Atlanta: Society of Biblical Literature, 2003.

Duran, Nicole Wilkinson. *Having Men for Dinner: Biblical Women's Deadly Banquets*. Cleveland: Pilgrim, 2006.

Exum, J. Cheryl. "Feminist Criticism: Whose Interests Are Being Served?" In *Judges and Method: New Approaches in Biblical Studies*, edited by Gale A. Yee, 65–90. Minneapolis: Fortress, 1995.

———. "'Mother in Israel': A Familiar Figure Reconsidered." In *Feminist Interpretation of the Bible*, edited by Letty M. Russell, 73–85. Philadelphia: Westminster, 1985.

Fischer, Stefan. "1 Samuel 28: The Woman of Endor—Who Is She and What Does Saul See?" *Old Testament Essays* 14 (2001) 26–46.

Fletcher, Joann. "From Warrior Women to Female Pharaohs: Careers for Women in Ancient Egypt." History. Ancient History. *BBC* (website), February 17, 2011. http://www.bbc.co.uk/history/ancient/egyptians/women_01.shtml/.

Fontaine, Carole R. *Smooth Words: Women, Proverbs, and Performance in Biblical Wisdom*. Journal for the Study of the Old Testament Supplement Series 356. London: Sheffield Academic, 2002.

Fox, Michael V. "The Women in Esther." *Torah.com* (website). 2015. https://thetorah.com/the-women-in-esther/.

Frymer-Kensky, Tikva. *In the Wake of the Goddesses: Women, Culture, and the Biblical Transformation of Pagan Myth*. New York: Ballantine, 1992.

———. *Studies in Bible and Feminist Criticism*. JPS Scholar of Distinction Series. Philadelphia: Jewish Publication Society, 2006.

Fuchs, Esther. "The Literary Characterization of Mothers & Sexual Politics in the Hebrew Bible." *Semeia* 46 (1989) 151–66.

———. "Prophecy and the Construction of Women." In *The Prophets and Daniel*, edited by Athalya Brenner-Idan, 54–69. Feminist Companion to the Bible, 2nd ser., 8. London: Sheffield Academic, 2001.

———. "Reclaiming the Hebrew Bible for Women: The Neoliberal Turn in Contemporary Feminist Scholarship." *Journal of Feminist Studies in Religion* 24/2 (2008) 45–65.

Gadotti, Alhena. "Mesopotamian Women's Cultic Roles in Late 3rd–Early 2nd Millennia BCE." In *Women in Antiquity: Real Women across the Ancient World*, edited by Stephanie Lynn Budin and Jean MacIntosh Turfa, 64–76. Rewriting Antiquity. London: Routledge, 2016.

Gansell, Amy Rebecca. "Women's Lives in the Ancient Near East and Facets of Ancient Near Eastern Womanhood." In *Women at the Dawn of History*, edited by Agnete W. Lassen and Klaus Wagensonner, 14–23. New Haven: Yale Babylonian Collection, Peabody Museum of Natural History, Yale University, 2020.

García Bachmann, Mercedes L. *Women at Work in the Deuteronomistic History*. International Voices in Biblical Studies 4. Atlanta: Society of Biblical Literature, 2013.

Genovés, Santiago. "Estimation of Age and Mortality." In *Science in Archaeology*, edited by Don Brothwell and Eric Higgs, 440–52. Revised and enlarged ed. London: Thames & Hudson, 1969.

Gillespie, Rosemary. "Childfree and Feminine: Understanding the Gender Identity of Voluntarily Childless Women." In *Gender and Society* 17 (2003) 122–36.

Goitein, S. D., and Michael Carasik. "Women as Creators of Biblical Genres." *Prooftexts* 8/1 (1988) 1–33.

Goldstein, Marcus S. "The Paleopathology of Human Skeletal Remains." In *Science in Archaeology*, edited by Don Brothwell and Eric Higgs, 480–89. Revised and enlarged ed. London: Thames & Hudson, 1969.

Gordon, Linda. *The Moral Property of Women: A History of Birth Control Politics in America*. 3rd ed. Urbana: University of Illinois Press, 2002.

Gosline, Sheldon L. "Female Priests: A Sacerdotal Precedent from Ancient Egypt." *Journal of Feminist Studies in Religion* 12/1 (1996) 25–39.

Halpern, Baruch. *The First Historians The Hebrew Bible and History*. San Francisco: Harper & Row, 1988.

Halton, Charles, and Saana Svärd, trans. and eds. *Women's Writing of Ancient Mesopotamia: An Anthology of the Earliest Female Authors*. Cambridge: Cambridge University Press, 2017.

Hamori, Esther J. "The Prophet and the Necromancer: Women's Divination for Kings." *Journal of Biblical Literature* 132 (2013) 827–43.

———. *Women's Divination in Biblical Literature: Prophecy, Necromancy, and Other Arts of Knowledge*. Anchor Yale Bible Reference Library. New Haven: Yale University Press, 2015.

Hancock, Rebecca S. "Esther and the Politics of Negotiation: An Investigation of Public and Private Spaces in Relationship to Possibilities for Female Royal Counselors." PhD diss., Harvard University, 2012.

Handy, Lowell K. "Reading Huldah as Being a Woman." *Biblical Research* 55 (2010) 5–44.

———. "The Role of Huldah in Josiah's Cult Reform." *Zeitschrift für die alttestamentliche Wissenschaft* 106 (2009) 40–53.

Haupt, Paul. "Moses' Song of Triumph." *American Journal of Semitic Languages and Literatures* 20 (April 1904) 149–72.

Havrelock, Rachel S. "The Myth of Birthing the Hero: Heroic Barrenness in the Hebrew Bible." *Biblical Interpretation* 16 (2008) 154–78.

Herzberg, Bruce. "Deborah and Moses." *Journal for the Study of the Old Testament* 38 (2013) 15–33. https://doi.org/10.1177%2F0309089213492816/.

Heschel, Abraham Joshua. *The Prophets*. Perennial Classics. New York: HarperPerennial, 2001.

Ilan, Tal. "Huldah, the Deuteronomic Prophetess of the Book of Kings." *Lectio Difficilior* 10/1 (2010) lectio.unibe.ch/10_1/ilan.html/.

Jackowski, Karol. "Holy Disobedience in Esther." *Theology Today* 45 (1989) 403–14.

Janssen, Rosalind M. "A New Reading of Shiphrah and Puah: Recovering Their Voices." *Feminist Theology* 27 (2018) 9–25.

Janzen, J. Gerald. "Song of Moses, Song of Miriam: Who Is Seconding Whom?" *Catholic Biblical Quarterly* 54 (1992) 211–20.

Kalmonofsky, Amy. "Israel's Baby: The Horror of Childbirth in the Biblical Prophets." *Biblical Interpretation* 16 (2008) 60–82.

Kamionkowski, Tamar. "Will the Real Miriam Please Stand Up?" *Torah.com* (website). 2015. https://thetorah.com/article/will-the-real-miriam-please-stand-up/.

Kohn, Leah. "The Woman of Tekoa: A Proper Use of Personal Talent." *Torah.org* (blog), June 24, 2020. https://torah.org/learning/women-class66/.

Labahn, Antje, and Ehud Ben Zvi. "Observations on Women in the Genealogies of 1 Chronicles 1–9." *Biblica* 84 (2003) 457–78.

Lahtinen, Sara. *The nadītum as Businesswoman: Economic Enterprise among Religiously Devoted Women in Old Babylonian Sippar.* Saarbrücken: Lambert Academic, 2011.

Lang, Bernhard. *Wisdom and the Book of Proverbs: A Hebrew Goddess Redefined.* New York: Pilgrim, 1986.

Lederman-Daniely, Dvora. "'I Arose a Mother in Israel': Motherhood as a Liberating Power in the Biblical Stories of Miriam and Deborah." In *Motherhood in Antiquity*, edited by Dana Cooper and Claire Phelan, 9–28. Cham, Switzerland: Springer, 2017.

———. "Revealing Miriam's Prophecy." *Feminist Theology* 25/1 (2016) 8–28.

Lockyer, Herbert. *All the Women of the Bible.* Grand Rapids: Zondervan, 1988.

Lubitch, Rivkah. "A Feminist's Look at Esther." *Judaism* 42 (1993) 438–46.

Lust, J. "On Wizards and Prophets." In *Studies on Prophecy: A Collection of Twelve Papers*, 133–42. Vetus Testamentum Supplement 26. Leiden: Brill, 1974. https://doi.org/10.1163/9789004275492_012/.

Luther, Martin. *The Table Talk of Martin Luther.* Edited with an introduction by Thomas S. Kepler. New York: Dover, 2005.

Mark, Joshua J. "Sammu-Ramat and Semiramis: The Inspiration and the Myth." In *Ancient History Encyclopedia.* September 16, 2014. https://www.ancient.eu/article/743/.

———. "Twelve Great Women of Ancient Persia." In *Ancient History Encyclopedia.* https://www.ancient.eu/article/1493/.

Marsman, Hennie J. *Women in Ugarit and Israel: Their Social and Religious Position in the Context of the Ancient Near East.* Oudtestamentische Studiën 49. Leiden: Brill, 2003.

McKinlay, Judith E. "Gazing at Huldah." *Bible and Critical Theory* 1/3 (2005) 1–11.

May, Natalie Naomi. "Female Scholars in Mesopotamia?." In *Gender and Methodology in the Ancient Near East: Approaches from Assyriology and Beyond*, edited by Stephanie Lynn Budin et al., 149–62. Barcelona: Edicions de la Universitat de Barcelona, 2018.

Meir, Tamar. "Miriam: Midrash and Aggadah." https://jwa.org/encyclopedia/article/miriam-midrash-and-aggadah/.

Meier, Samuel A. "Women and Communication in The Ancient Near East." *Journal of the American Oriental Society* 3 (1991) 540–47.

Meyers, Carol. "The Roots of Restriction: Women in Early Israel." *Biblical Archaeologist* 41 (1978) 91–103.

———. "Women with Hand-Drums, Dancing: Bible." *The Encyclopedia of Jewish Women* https://jwa.org/encyclopedia/article/women-with-hand-drums-dancing-bible/.

———. "Women's Religious Life (Iron Age Israel)." In *Women in Antiquity: Real Women across the Ancient World*, edited by Stephanie Lynn Budin and Jean MacIntosh Turfa, 511–20. Rewriting Antiquity. London: Routledge, 2016.

Michael, Matthew. "Narrative Conjuring or the Tales of Two Sisters? The Representations of Hannah and the Witch of Endor in 1 Samuel." *Journal for the Study of the Old Testament* 42 (2018) 469–89.

Miller, Robert D., II. "The Witch at the Navel of the World." *Zeitschrift für die alttestamentliche Wissenschaft* 129 (2017) 98–102. https://doi.org/10.1515/zaw-201 7-0008/.

Mohler, Albert. "Deliberate Childlessness: Moral Rebellion with a New Face." http://albertmohler.com/commentary_read.php?cdate=200 4-0 6-28/.

Moore, Carey A. *Esther*. Anchor Bible 7B. Garden City, NY: Doubleday, 1971.

Mwendambio, Paluku. "Depiction of the Status of Women in Israel during the Iron Age." Unpublished manuscript, 2008.

Nakhai, Beth Alpert. "Factors Complicating the Reconstruction of Women's Lives in Iron Age Israel (1200–587 B.C.E.)." In *Studying Gender in the Ancient Near East*, edited by Saana Svärd and Agnès Garcia-Ventura, 289–313. University Park, PA: Eisenbrauns, 2018.

———. "Gender and Archaeology in Israelite Religion." *Compass Religion* 1 (2007) 512–28.

———. "Women in Israelite Religion: The State of Research Is All New Research." *Religions* 10/2 (2019) 122. https://doi.org/10.3390/.

Niditch, Susan. "Legends of Wise Heroes and Heroines." In *The Hebrew Bible and Its Modern Interpreters*, edited by Douglas A. Knight and Gene M. Tucker, 445–63. The Bible and Its Modern Interpreters 1. Centennial Publications of the Society of Biblical Literature. Chico, CA: Scholars, 1985.

Nissinen, Martti. *Ancient Prophecy: Near Eastern, Biblical, and Greek Perspectives*. Oxford: Oxford University Press, 2017.

Olojede, Funlola. "Women and the Cry for Justice in Old Testament Court Narratives: An African Reflection." *Old Testament Essays* 26 (2013) 761–72.

Paz, Sarit. *Drums, Women, and Goddesses: Drumming and Gender in Iron Age II Israel*. Orbis biblicus et orientalis 232. Göttingen: Vanderhoek & Ruprecht, 2007.

Peck, Ellen, and Judith Senderowitz, eds. *Pronatalism: The Myth of Mom & Apple Pie*. New York: Crowell, 1974.

Picton, Jan. "Living and Working in a New Kingdom 'Harem Town.'" In *Women in Antiquity: Real Women across the Ancient World*, edited by Stephanie Lynn Budin and Jean MacIntosh Turfa, 229–42. Rewriting Antiquity. London: Routledge, 2016.

Pierce, Ronald W. "Deborah: Troublesome Woman or Woman of Valor?" *Priscilla Papers* 32 (2008) 3–7. https://www.cbeinternational.org/resource/article/priscilla-papers-academic-journal/deborah-troublesome-woman-or-woman-valor/.

Pigott, Susan M. "Wives, Witches, and Wise Women: Prophetic Heralds of Kingship in 1 and 2 Samuel." *Review and Expositor* 99 (2002) 145–73. https://doi.org/10.1177/0 03463730209900203.

Priest, John. "Huldah's Oracle." *Vetus Testamentum* 30 (1980) 366–68.

Reinhartz, Adele "Anonymity and Character in the Books of Samuel." *Semeia* 63 (1993) 117–41.

Reis, Pamela Tamarkin. "Eating the Blood: Saul and the Witch of Endor." *Journal for the Study of the Old Testament* 22/73 (1997) 3–23. https://doi.org/10.1177/0309089297 02207301/.

Riddle, John M., et al. "Ever Since Eve . . . Birth Control in the Ancient World." *Archaeology* 47/2 (1994) 29–35.

Ruane, Nicole J. "When Women Are Not Enough." In *Feminist Interpretation of the Hebrew Bible in Retrospect*, edited by Susanne Scholz, 3:243–60. 3 vols. Recent Research in Biblical Studies 5, 8–9. Sheffield: Sheffield Phoenix, 2016.

Sakenfeld, Katharine Doob. "Numbers." In *Women's Bible Commentary*, edited by Carol A. Newsom and Sharon H. Ringe, 49–56. Exp. ed. Louisville: Westminster John Knox, 1998.

Sasson, Jack. "'A Breeder or Two for Each Leader': On Mothers in Judges 4 and 5." In *A Critical Engagement: Essays on the Hebrew Bible in Honour of J. Cheryl Exum*, edited by David J. A. Clines and Ellen van Wolde, 333–54. Sheffield, England: Sheffield Phoenix, 2012.

Schneider, Tammi J. *Judges*. Berit Olam. Collegeville, MN: Liturgical, 2000.

Schnur, Susan. "The Womantasch Triangle: Vashti, Esther, and Carol Gilligan." *Lillith* (1998). https://www.lilith.org/articles/tne-womantasch-triangle/.

Schwartz, Earl. "The Wisdom of Women." *Reconstructionist* 55/3 (1990) 11–24.

Siegel, Ben. "The Necromancer's Inheritance: The Ba'alat Ov of Endor in 1 Samuel 28." https://www.academia.edu/2031390/The_Necromancer_s_Inheritance_The_Ba_alat_Ov_of_Endor_in_1_Samuel_28/.

Simon, Uriel. "A Balanced Story: The Stern Prophet and the Kind Witch." *Prooftexts* 8 (1988) 159–71. https://www.jstor.org/stable/20689207.

Skidmore-Hess, Daniel, and Cathy Skidmore-Hess. "Dousing the Fiery Woman: The Diminishing of the Prophetess Deborah." *Shofar* 31/1 (2012) 1–17.

Song, Angeline. "Heartless Bimbo or Subversive Role Model? A Narrative (Self) Critical Reading of the Character of Esther." *Dialog* 49 (2010) 56–69.

Stanton, Elizabeth Cady. *The Original Feminist Attack on the Bible (The Woman's Bible).* With an introduction by Barbara Welter. New York: Amo, 1974.

Stein, David. "What Does It Mean to Be a 'Man'? The Noun *'ish* in Biblical Hebrew: A Reconsideration." 2006. http://scholar.davidesstein.name/Memoranda.htm/.

Stökl, Jonathan, and Corrine L. Carvalho. *Prophets Male and Female: Gender and Prophecy in the Hebrew Bible, the Eastern Mediterranean, and the Ancient Near East*. Ancient Israel and Its Literature. Atlanta: Society of Biblical Literature, 2013.

Stol, Marten. *Birth in Babylonia and the Bible: Its Mediterranean Setting*. Cuneiform Monographs 14. Groningen: Styx, 2000.

———. *Women in the Ancient Near East*. Translated by Helen and Mervyn Richardson. Berlin: de Gruyter, 2016.

Stone, Ken. "Gender Criticism: The Un-manning of Abimelech." In *Judges & Method: New Approaches in Biblical Studies*, edited by Gale A. Yee,183–201. 2nd ed. Minneapolis: Fortress, 2007.

Stone, Meredith J. *Empire and Gender in LXX Esther*. Early Judaism and Its Literature 48. Atlanta: SBL Press, 2018.

Stuckey, Johanna H. "Priestesses and 'Sacred Prostitutes.'" *Canadian Woman Studies les Cahiers De La Femme* 17 (1997) 6–9.

Swidler, Arlene. "In Search of Huldah." *Bible Today* 98 (1978) 1780–85.

Tamber-Rosenau, Caryn. "The 'Mothers' Who Were Not: Motherhood Imagery and Childless Women Warriors in Early Jewish Literature." In *Mothers in the Jewish Cultural Imagination*, edited by Marjorie Lehman et al., 185–206. Jewish Cultural Studies 5. Liverpool: The Littman Library of Jewish Civilization, in association with Liverpool University Press, 2017.

———. "Striking Women: Performance and Gender in the Hebrew Bible and Early Jewish Literature." PhD diss. Vanderbilt University, 2015.

Taylor, J Glen. "The Song of Deborah and Two Canaanite Goddesses." *Journal for the Study of the Old Testament* 23 (1982) 99–108.

Teubal, Savina J. *Sarah the Priestess: The First Matriarch of Genesis*. Athens, OH: Swallow, 1984.

Thimmes, Pamela. "What Makes a Feminist Reading Feminist? Another Perspective." In *Escaping Eden: New Feminist Perspectives on the Bible*, edited by Harold C. Washington et al., 132–40. New York: New York University Press, 1999.

Toorn, Karel van der. *Scribal Culture and the Making of the Hebrew Bible*. Cambridge: Harvard University Press, 2007.

Trible, Phyllis. "Huldah's Holy Writ: On Women and Biblical Authority." *Touchstone* 3 (1985) 6–13.

Webb, Barry G. *The Book of the Judges: An Integrated Reading*. Journal for the Study of the Old Testament Supplement Series 46. Sheffield, England: Sheffield Academic, 1987.

Westermann, Claus. *Basic Forms of Prophetic Speech*. Translated by Hugh Clayton White. With a new foreword by Gene M. Tucker. Louisville: Westminster John Knox, 1991.

Wills, Lawrence M. *The Jewish Novel in the Ancient World*. Myth and Poetics. Ithaca: Cornell University Press, 1995.

Wilson, Ellie. "Anat: Autonomous Goddess of Ugarit." Paper presented at Society of Biblical Literature Annual Meeting, Washington DC, November 1993. https://heartwellproductions.wordpress.com/anat-autonomous-goddess-of-ugarit/.

Wilson, Robert R. *Prophecy and Society in Ancient Israel*. Philadelphia: Fortress, 1980.

Van Wyk, Susandra J. "Prostitute, Nun or 'Man-Woman': Revisiting the Position of the Old Babylonian Nadiātu Priestesses." *Journal of Northwest Semitic Languages* 41 (2015) 95–122.

Yee, Gale A. "By the Hand of a Woman: The Metaphor of the Woman Warrior in Judges 4." *Semeia* (1993) 99–132.

Zahavi-Ely, Naama. "'Turn Right or Left': Literary Use of Dialect in 2 Samuel 14:19?" *Hebrew Studies* 53 (2012) 43–53. https://www.jstor.org/stable/23344439/.

Zucker, David J. "Entertaining Esther: Vamp, Victim, and Virtuous Woman." *Women in Judaism* 9/2 (2012) 1–12. https://wjudaism.library.utoronto.ca/index.php/wjudaism/article/view/19255/.

———. "The Importance of Being Esther: Rabbis, Canonicity, Problems and Possibilities." *European Judaism* 47 (2014) 102–8.

SCRIPTURE INDEX